Praise for *The Witches' Sabbath*

"Kelden leads the reader through a wealth of well-selected and fully-referenced stories from history, folklore, and art, from American and European sources, to provide a solid foundation for understanding the concept of the Witches' Sabbath as it has developed over the centuries. The academic material, which is presented in an accessible and readable style, is combined with useful, practical information for the modern practitioner wishing to explore the Witches' Sabbath for themselves."

—Val Thomas, author of *Of Chalk and Flint: A Way of Norfolk Magic*

"In this well-researched and fascinating book, Kelden provides readers with an accessible and engaging academic history of the Witches' Sabbath and also with a practical, hands-on manual for any magical practitioner, novice or adept, to journey there themselves. This book contains the historical context and folkloric imagery that modern practitioners can be inspired by along with realistic step-by-step instructions for understanding and equipping for a journey over the hedge and into spirit flight."

—Dodie Graham McKay, author of *Earth Magic*

"*The Witch's Sabbath* is by far the best resource on the history and practice of the witch's flight. Kelden has documented numerous records of Witches and their spirit travels—from the women who flew alongside the goddess Diana to the people who confessed during the inquisitions and trials, and all the way into the modern age with his own experiences. The reader is given a wealth of information, including the various kinds of spirits and activities that occur at these Otherworldly rites. He also provides helpful information to prepare the reader to make the voyage, which may seem impossible until you've actually done it."

—Astrea Taylor, author of *Intuitive Witchcraft and Air Magic*

T0054078

"Carefully wading through the history of Witch flight, ecstasy, shapeshifting, familiar forms, flying ointments and more, Kelden guides us on thrilling journeys over the hedge and through the Otherworld. Readers will learn to create their own broom, feast with the spirits, dance with the Otherworldly, and develop their practice utilizing traditional techniques of magical art for the modern day. *The Witches' Sabbath* has already become a go-to guide in my library and inspired change in my art."

—Via Hedera, author of *Folkloric American Witchcraft and the Multicultural Experience*

"This book provides a comprehensive, compact, and accurate survey of traditional beliefs surrounding the Witches' sabbath and a practical introduction to an interesting and distinctive operative modern tradition which enacts them."

—Professor Ronald Hutton, English historian at the University of Bristol

THE
WITCHES'
SABBATH

About the Author

Kelden (Minnesota) has been practicing Traditional Witchcraft for more than a decade. He is the author of *The Crooked Path: An Introduction to Traditional Witchcraft*. Additionally, his writing has appeared in *The Witch's Altar*, *The New Aradia: A Witch's Handbook to Magical Resistance*, and *This Witch* magazine. Kelden is also the cocreator of *The Traditional Witch's Deck*, and he authors a blog on the Patheos Pagan channel called *By Athame and Stang*. In his free time, Kelden enjoys reading, hiking, growing poisonous plants, and playing ukulele.

WITCHES' THE SABBATH

An EXPLORATION of HISTORY, FOLKLORE & MODERN PRACTICE

KELDEN

Llewellyn Publications
Woodbury, Minnesota

FIRST EDITION
First Printing, 2022

Cover design by Kevin R. Brown
Cover illustration by Tim Foley
Figure illustration by Wen Hsu, all other art by Llewellyn Art Department

Llewellyn Publications is a registered trademark of Llewellyn Worldwide Ltd.

Library of Congress Cataloging-in-Publication Data
Names: Kelden, author.
Title: The Witches' Sabbath : an exploration of history, folklore & modern
    practice / Kelden.
Description: Woodbury, Minnesota : Llewellyn Publications, 2022. | Includes
    bibliographical references. | Summary: "History, lore, and traditions of
    the Witches' Sabbath, a gathering described in confessions of accused
    Witches throughout their historical persecution and attended today by
    modern practitioners in physical or astral form"— Provided by
    publisher.
Identifiers: LCCN 2021041680 (print) | LCCN 2021041681 (ebook) | ISBN
    9780738767116 (paperback) | ISBN 9780738767178 (ebook)
Subjects: LCSH: Walpurgis Night. | Witchcraft. | Wicca.
Classification: LCC BF1572.W35 K45 2022 (print) | LCC BF1572.W35 (ebook)
    | DDC 133.4/3—dc23
LC record available at https://lccn.loc.gov/2021041680
LC ebook record available at https://lccn.loc.gov/2021041681

Llewellyn Publications
A Division of Llewellyn Worldwide Ltd.
2143 Wooddale Drive
Woodbury, MN 55125-2989
www.llewellyn.com

Printed in the United States of America

Also by Kelden

The Crooked Path: An Introduction to Traditional Witchcraft

To my sister, Breanna.
Thank you for teaching me the magic of writing.

Acknowledgments

First and foremost, much thanks and gratitude to the team at Llewellyn for believing in me and my writing. Thank you especially to my fabulous editors. Heather, thank you for taking on this project and for helping me to refine my mad mind rambles. Lauryn, as always, you have gone above and beyond helping me with grammar and citations—thank you so much for going down so many research rabbit holes with me!

Of course, none of this would ever be possible without the love and encouragement from my family—Dad, Mom, Breanna, and Colton. A special thanks to my grandma Pearl for fostering a family legacy of book lovers. Hail the traveler! Thank you to my dear friends Veles, Thorn, Marina, Sara, Jane, and Philip for always lending a sympathetic ear and talking me through the plights of imposter syndrome. Thank you to the magical baristas at Coffee Talk—David, Luke, and Steven—for keeping me sufficiently caffeinated during the writing process. A huge thank you to the force of nature that is Jason Mankey, someone who I have always viewed as an incredible writer and a personal inspiration—thank you so much for providing the foreword for this book and for being a fellow Witchcraft history nerd.

Finally, as always, thank you to the black spirits of the north, the red spirits of the east, the green spirits of the south, and the blue spirits of the west. Thank you to the spirits above and the spirits below, the spirits of the land, and the Fair Folk. Thank you to the Witch Father and Witch Mother, my ancestors, and my familiar spirit.

Disclaimer

The information contained in this book derives from historical and folkloric sources as well as from personal experience. It is no way meant to replace qualified medical care, including that provided by mental health professionals. The author and publisher are not liable for any injury or ill-effect caused by the application of information provided in this book. Do not ingest poisonous or unfamiliar plants, and take care when handling them. Please use your common sense when utilizing any of the practices discussed, and consult the advice of a trained medical practitioner when necessary.

Trigger Warning

The following book contains historical and folkloric references to several topics that may be upsetting to some readers, including mentions of infanticide, cannibalism, and incest. If you are someone who may be triggered by such topics, unfortunately this book will not be for you.

Contents

FOREWORD

My first-ever Witch ritual with other people or entities occurred on a Midsummer night in the backseat of my father's car. I had gone with my dad and some of his friends to an out-of-town concert on the summer solstice. On the ride home I closed my eyes and found myself somewhere *else*. That somewhere else wasn't like the Sabbat (seasonal celebration) rituals I'd read about in Wiccan Witchcraft books—it was a place full of Otherworldly Witches and spirits. That elsewhere I visited felt as if it were outside of known time and space and that the visitors there could have been from any time period or place. Without thinking about it, or really trying to get there, I had visited the legendary Witches' Sabbath, a Witchcraft experience like no other. Years later as I began making friends in the greater Witchcraft community, I would bring up my experiences in this other world. Some of those Witches looked at me in bewilderment, while others nodded along and began finishing my sentences for me. I was surprised to find that other Witches had visited the same place I had and that our experiences were similar.

The Witches' Sabbath is a topic that comes up a lot in Witchcraft books, but it's rarely elaborated upon. Over the last fifty years, it's become fashionable to write about Witchcraft in a way that makes it feel safe and wholesome to outsiders. Such descriptions dull the sharp edges of Witchcraft down to rounded corners and exclude anything that might make the neighbors uncomfortable. During the era of Satanic Panic (from the mid-1970s through the early 1990s), perhaps that was an advisable strategy in public spaces, but it makes for a much more boring and less vibrant Witchcraft.

Hundreds of years ago, those accused of Witchcraft were often the most vulnerable and marginalized members of society. Those accused Witches, who were predominantly women, were scorned for owning their sexuality, practicing magic, and disrupting the social order. Not everyone accused of Witchcraft was executed, but death was a punishment handed out to tens of thousands. Even the simple accusation of Witchcraft could have serious repercussions: homelessness, financial hardship, and loss of family and friends. Many of those tortured and accused of Witchcraft confessed to attending what would become known as the Witches' Sabbath. At the Sabbath, individuals were free to own their sexual selves, indulge in magical practice, dance, feast, and do the other things that make life worth living. Confessions derived from torture are always suspect, but it seems to me that these alleged Witches were most certainly going *somewhere*. The Sabbath was an escape, a place to revel in the idealized self with everyone else present in that space willing to accept you.

There is often a very large disconnect between contemporary Witches and those who were executed during the Witch Trials. Many modern scholars scoff at suggestions that today's Craft has origins in the more distant past, but I'm not sure such theories can be discounted entirely. While it's unlikely that there is an unbroken chain connecting my Witchcraft beliefs with victims of the Witch Trials four hundred years ago, there are most certainly connections. There was an edge to their descriptions of the Witches' Sabbath both then and now, an edge that inspires and provokes. And it's undeniable that the stories told about the Sabbath by those accused of Witchcraft centuries ago continue to influence our Craft today.

I have always felt as if Witchcraft were a journey and not a destination, and you'll go on a variety of journeys in this book. You'll find yourself connecting to Witches of long ago while also getting swept up in tales about the Fair Folk, familiar spirits, and even the Devil himself. You'll explore numinous Sabbath locations and witness strange dancing and magic making. There are contemporary stops too, visits with often-over-looked Witchcraft pioneers such as Austin Osman Spare and Andrew Chumbley. And you'll come to see just how the Witches' Sabbath came to exist in the modern practices of both Traditional Witchcraft and Wicca.

Beyond history and folklore, Kelden shares the many paths that can take the modern Witch on their very own journey to the Sabbath. The elsewhere can be reached by expanding our consciousness, or perhaps softening our mundane minds with an elixir or the legendary Witches' ointment. By treading the Witches' mill, we can use our physical bodies to help us reach another state of consciousness and a different reality. To be a Witch is to traverse the space between worlds and all who inhabit such liminal spaces. Many who seek the Witches' Sabbath stumble blindly into it, unaware of the space they are entering. There are also those who write about the Sabbath like a closely guarded secret, whispering about the path while refusing to provide a road map. In this book, Kelden doesn't just provide a road map; he gives you a guided tour. The Sabbath can be accessed by anyone, alone or with friends, regardless of specific tradition or level of experience. The keys to this journey are all present in this book. It's simply a matter of picking them up and having the mind to use them.

For some Witches, history can be boring, but there's nothing boring to be found in this book. Kelden's *The Witches' Sabbath* is one of the best Witchcraft journeys I've been on in quite some time. The size and scope of the journey are epic, and I believe that reading this book will make you a better Witch. Witches have traditionally always been the "others," the people who refuse to conform to society's parameters and are comfortable in their own (and other) skins. The Witches' Sabbath is a place to indulge in that otherness with others who also embrace it. No matter how you get to the Sabbath, you'll find a home and a power there. It's a journey worth taking.

Jason W. Mankey
July 2021

INTRODUCTION

On the night of Walpurga, a lone Witch approaches their fireplace with a quiet knowing. The embers have cooled and turned to ash, leaving the hearth both still and silent, with the exception of a ticking clock sitting upon the mantle. The hour approaches midnight. Removing the cork from a small clay pot, the Witch dips the fingers of their left hand into an ointment that gives off a pungent earthy aroma. With concentrated movements, the Witch rubs the sticky salve onto their wrists, behind their ears, and upon the soles of their feet. Then, mounting a broomstick that had previously been resting against the gray stone fireplace, the Witch closes their eyes and utters the words "Thout, tout a tout, tout, throughout and about." And with a whoosh, they are carried up the chimney and out into the night.

The wind howls as the Witch soars across the darkened sky, an inky black tapestry devoid of the stars and moon, which have been obscured by thick clouds. The Witch flies over the tops of houses, where inhabitants sleep restlessly, their heads filled with strange dreams. Farther and farther the Witch journeys, over city walls and into the wild countryside where few dare to go. Higher and higher they travel, up the side of a looming mountain that has the reputation of being haunted by ghosts and faeries. Finally, reaching the summit, the Witch touches down upon the ground in the middle of a clearing, where others have already started to gather around a roaring bonfire.

The boisterous scene that unfolds before the Witch's eyes is both awe-inspiring and frightening. Around the fire, which has an unearthly greenish glow, other

Witches dance in a ring with their backs to the flames. The strange dance is set to the tune of an eerie song played on flutes and tambourines. Additional Witches sit nearby, crafting dolls and mixing powders, preparing these items for the working of spells. Still other Witches are gathered around a long banquet table, feasting upon bread and wine. Enthroned at the head of the gathering is a man dressed all in black, the Devil. He watches over the Witches as they revel in his honor, each act one of empowerment for both the Witches and himself. Shedding all of their mundane worry and stress and casting off their mortal inhibitions, the Witch joins the festivities, which will continue until the rooster crows, announcing the arrival of dawn.

The above story describes the events of what is known as the *Witches' Sabbath*, a nocturnal meeting between Witches and the Devil. Growing up, I enjoyed nothing more than reading stories about Witches, both fictional and historical. A common theme that I came to find in these tales was the idea that practitioners of the Craft convened together on special nights in some secret location. Of course, depending upon the source, these meetings ranged from relatively benign to outright diabolical. In one story, the Sabbath could be presented as a quaint—albeit spooky—assembly, while in another it was shown to be barbaric and grotesquely evil. Either way, there was something incredibly alluring about these Sabbath gatherings, something that pulled at my spirit and whispered encouragingly for me to come along.

When I first started learning about the practice of modern Witchcraft, specifically Wicca, I was taught about the *sabbats*. In Wicca and some other Neopagan paths, the sabbats are celebratory rituals (known collectively as the *Wheel of Year*) that focus on connecting to deities as they are reflected in the changing seasonal tides. However, while these sabbats are a contemporary conceptualization, they are based in part on older folklore regarding those same nocturnal Witch meetings I had read about as a child. As my personal practice as a Witch shifted over the years and I became more interested in what is known as *Traditional Witchcraft* (a non-Wiccan form of Craft), I started to reconsider the folklore of the Sabbath and how it could be applied to my modern practice. The book that you are about to read is the culmination of my years of research on, as well as my own experiences of journeying to, the Witches' Sabbath.

It's important to note up front that the material within this book—particularly that relating to modern practice—will be presented through the specific lens of Traditional Witchcraft. Within Traditional Craft, practitioners view the Sabbath as an Otherworldly gathering of Witches and assorted spirits. While there are ways in which the Sabbath can be enacted in physical space (which will be touched upon in chapter 8), the primary focus of the discussions on modern application in this book will be on the Sabbath as a spectral event—one that requires the solitary Witch to travel into the Otherworld. Therefore, while the Wiccan Wheel of Year will be discussed in terms of its relationship to the overarching historical development of the Witches' Sabbath, please be aware that this is not intended to be a book about Wicca nor the seasonal holidays celebrated within that distinct branch of the Craft. That being said, although the chapters pertaining to modern application will be rooted in Traditional Witchcraft, anyone can make use of the beliefs and practices found therein, regardless of their tradition.

The book itself is structured with chapters dedicated alternately to the historical and folkloric background of the Witches' Sabbath and to modern practice. In order to further illustrate the Sabbath's nature, I have included extra sections entitled "The Sabbath in Art." As the name suggests, in these sections you'll find examinations of the Sabbath as it has appeared in various forms of art throughout time. Additionally, there are several exercises within the book—including recipes, spells, and rituals—that will aid you in your own journey to the Witches' Sabbath. At the end of the book is an appendix containing a list of the many accused Witches mentioned, including their geographic location and the date they were either tried or executed, for quick and easy reference. Furthermore, in the back of the book you'll also find a glossary, bibliography, and recommended reading list.

Witch Trial Transcripts

In discussing the Witches' Sabbath, I will be frequently citing the confessions of those individuals who were accused of Witchcraft across Europe and in the early American colonies. In mentioning these cases, I am in no way attempting to suggest that the accused were actual practitioners of Witchcraft. We know today that most confessions were obtained under torture, during which individuals would have confessed to just about anything in order to escape pain and death. Additionally, others were subjected to sleep deprivation and other hostile conditions, under which both their physical and mental health would have rapidly deteriorated. Interrogators were also guilty of using leading questions and other techniques in order to manipulate the narrative to fit their own agenda. Finally, confessions were not always recorded verbatim, and later translations were susceptible to being distorted—sometimes even intentionally so.

That being said, while those accused were most likely innocent wholesale, the fact remains that many of the details presented in their confessions—whether given by the accused or inserted by interrogators—reflected pre-established beliefs regarding the practice of Witchcraft. Author Emma Wilby notes that when it comes to the confessions given by the accused, "We must assume that when crafting their accounts of benign akelarre [Sabbath] festivities, suspects drew on the gossip and propaganda surrounding the nocturnal meetings of witches that circulated in the region both before and during the witch prosecution."[1] Thus, confessional statements can be mined as repositories of folk beliefs, in this case those that pertain specifically to the Witches' Sabbath. And examination of trial transcripts allows us, as present-day practitioners, to better understand the ways in which the accounts given by the accused inadvertently influenced the development of modern Witchcraft. Additionally, such explorations also provide us with a wealth of lore that can help further inspire our practice as Witches moving forward.

---

1. Emma Wilby, *Invoking the Akelarre: Voices of the Accused in the Basque Witch-Craze, 1609–1614* (Chicago: Sussex Academic Press, 2019), 182–83.

Countries Discussed

In this book, I will be taking a multiregional approach, discussing the Sabbath as it appeared in various different countries. As noted before, this will include several European countries as well as the early American colonies. The concept of nocturnal assemblies of Witches emerged in many diverse places, and those discussed in this text are by no means an exhaustive list. Certain countries are not mentioned herein due to either an absence of Sabbath stories or a scarcity of documentation regarding the trials that took place in those regions. As you read, you may also notice that some countries are talked about at length while others are only briefly considered. The cause of this discrepancy lies in the amount of details given in certain places, which was smaller in some while larger in others. For example, the accounts of English Sabbaths were quite scanty in comparison to those found in France and Spain.

Chapter 1
STOKING THE SABBATH FIRE

Throughout time and across cultures, there have always been Witches in one form or another—individuals with magical powers that were typically used in order to cause harm to those within the Witches' community. Through their wicked words and detestable deeds, Witches could bring about illness, blight local crops, or cause other assorted disasters. As such, they have always presented a sort of danger to society at large, a shroud of menace that threatened to poison the daily lives of godly folk. However, for a long time Witches were seen as solitary practitioners who went about their dark arts alone. But by the time the first wave of European Witch Trials started (approximately the fifteenth century), terrifying ideas had begun to emerge regarding large groups of Witches who would fly through the dead of night to diabolical meetings with the Devil. These nocturnal gatherings, which would become a central element in many trials, involved a host of nefarious activities, such as demon worship, casting of spells for harm, feasting on the flesh of infants, and wild orgies. This coming together of Witches and the Devil has been referred to by many names throughout history and folklore, from generic terms such as *assembly* to more specific ones such as *synagogue*. However, the name that has stuck the longest, and that which people are most familiar with today, is *Sabbath*.

From a modern vantage point, the Sabbath is a relatively tidy, well-defined construct, like an intricately woven tapestry full of rich detail.

But like a tapestry, the imagery of the Witches' Sabbath was woven out of many disparate threads, and that was a process that occurred gradually over time. Much to the chagrin of researchers (myself included), there is no clear point of origin for the Witches' Sabbath, no distinct moment in time when the concept was sparked into existence. Despite its unknown exact moment of creation, the notion of the Witches' Sabbath emerged during the Middle Ages from a mixture of ecclesiastical ideas regarding demonology fused with elements of early paganism that had been preserved in popular folklore. Rather than being a monolithic entity, in the beginning the Sabbath was more of a loose framework upon which assorted regional and cultural elements would be added over time. The end result, and what we are left with today, is vividly detailed stories regarding Witches gathering in the night to work their evil spells and pay homage to the Devil. But, in order to have a well-rounded understanding of these tales and the role they play in today's practice of Witchcraft, we must determine how their basic structure was first composed. To do so, it will be necessary to dismantle the narrative as it's known today and to examine all the individual parts. Thus, to truly comprehend what would become known as the Witches' Sabbath we must start by pulling out the threads of history and folklore and unravel the tapestry altogether.

Etymology of the Witches' Sabbath

It is often said that knowing the true name of something gives you power over it. Whether or not this is true, knowing the origins of a word certainly gives you valuable insight into what it describes. Thus, before we become fully immersed in its developmental history, it will serve us well to examine the specific etymology of the term *Witches' Sabbath*. The word *Sabbath* is one that has long been associated with both Judaism and Christianity, specifically referring to their holy day of the week. The word derives from the Latin *sabbatum*, the Greek *sabbaton*, and the Hebrew *shabbath*—all meaning "day of rest."[2] Traditionally, this period of rest

---

2. Online Etymology Dictionary, "Sabbath (*n.*)," accessed February 5, 2021, https://www
    .etymonline.com/word/Sabbath#etymonline_v_22557.

occurred on the seventh day of the week, or Saturday. According to the book of Genesis, it was on the seventh day that God rested after he finished creating the world. But this only begs the question, how did a term that's been classically used to describe a holy day for both Jews and Christians come to be associated with the gathering of Witches?

The specific term *Witches' Sabbath* is actually of quite obscure origin and, to this day, a secure provenance remains absent. One of the earliest documented uses of the term *Sabbath* in connection to *Witches* reportedly occurred in the trial account of a French woman, Jehanne Guerme, in 1446. Sixteen years later, in 1462, the term *Sabbath* again appeared in Petrus Mamoris's *Flagellum maleficorum*.[3] However, the use of Sabbath as the name for gatherings of Witches wouldn't become popularly used until the late sixteenth century and onward. Prior to this, Witch meetings were referred to by many other names, including *assemblies, convents,* and *synagogues.* The use of the latter term, which has historically been used to describe congregations of Jewish people, reveals an early prejudiced belief that Judaism was a form of both heresy and Witchcraft. And, as will be seen shortly, the persecution of Jewish people during the early Middle Ages actually played a key role in the budding development of the Witches' Sabbath narrative.

An additional explanation for the use of the word *Sabbath* to describe gatherings of Witches was hinted at by the French jurist and political theorist Jean Bodin. In his influential 1580 book, *De la démonomanie des sorciers*, Bodin wrote that Saturday was a day sanctified by God. But, in a strange twist, it was also on this night that God supposedly gave permission to evil spirits to chastise and harm people. Bodin went on to add that Saturday belonged to the planet Saturn, which was long held to possess malefic power. It is of interest to note, as Bodin pointed out, that the Hebrew word for Saturn is *Shabtai*, which itself is associated with the

---

3. Martine Ostorero, "The Concept of the Witches' Sabbath in the Alpine Region (1430–1440): Text and Context," in *Witchcraft Mythologies and Persecutions*, vol. 3 of *Demons, Spirits, Witches*, eds. Gábor Klaniczay and Éva Pócs (New York: Central European University Press, 2008), 28.

word *shabat* or *sabbath*.[4] However, as we will discuss in chapter 3, the date of the Witches' Sabbath was highly varied and its occurrence was by no means exclusive to Saturday nights. Yet another prominent suggestion has been that the Witches' Sabbath as a whole was an inverse, or at least partial inverse, of the Christian faith. In this case, it would appear that the particular date didn't matter as much as the specific diabolical events that took place therein. It was those details that were most interesting to the persecutors and writers of the time. In this sense, the term *Sabbath* was used rather liberally to describe any coming together of Witches, regardless of the specific day of the week. And by the late sixteenth century onward, *Sabbath* became the common word used to denote these sorcerous convocations.

Early Accusations

As we embark on our exploration of the historical development of the Witches' Sabbath, we must start with a discussion on a rather surprising topic—the accusations made by Roman pagans against the early Christians. During the first century and onward, as Christianity began to grow, the Roman people viewed its practices with a great deal of suspicion. Out of those suspicions, whispered rumors and accusations started to circulate. It was said that Christians regularly came together in the night to participate in three unforgivably heinous acts: infanticide, cannibalism, and incestuous orgies. Out of all possible crimes, those three were likely cited in particular due to ways in which they are monstrously antithetical to both civilized humanity and nature itself. There is reason to believe that those damaging stereotypes were already in place by 112 CE, as the Younger Pliny wrote about Christians defending themselves against unnamed rumors regarding their religious meetings.[5] Perhaps the most detailed account of the early accusations against Christians comes from

---

4. Jean Bodin, *On the Demon-Mania of Witches*, trans. Randy A. Scott (Toronto: Centre for Reformation and Renaissance Studies, 1995), 150–51.

5. Younger Pliny, *The Letters of the Younger Pliny*, trans. John B. Firth, 2nd series (London: Walter Scott, 1900), 270–72.

the *Octavius*, which was written by a man named Marcus Minucius Felix sometime around the end of the second century.

The text was written in the form of a conversation between a pagan named Caecilius Natalis and a Christian named Octavius Januarius. In chapter 9, Caecilius argued against Christianity by citing several rumors he'd heard about its adherents. He described how Christians supposedly adored the severed head of an ass, which he noted was considered the most abject of animals. Additionally, Caecilius commented on how it was believed that Christians worshiped the genitals of their priests. Both of these acts were a part of the religion's secret, nocturnal rites alongside a grizzly initiation ceremony involving the murder and cannibalization of an infant. Specifically, a new Christian would be required to repeatedly stab a pile of dough in which the other members had concealed a baby. Together, the congregants would then feast upon the infant's body. Finally, Caecilius detailed how the entire diabolical gathering had been illuminated by a singular lamp, to which a dog had been tied. Toward the end of the meeting a scrap of food was tossed just beyond the reach of said dog who, in its attempt to obtain the morsel, would subsequently overturn the lamp. The room would be plunged into total darkness, and it was at that point that indiscriminate sexual activity, including incest, commenced.[6]

The accusations and stereotypes, such as those presented in *Octavius*, would go on to help fuel the persecution of early Christians up until the fourth century—at which point Christianity took over and became the official religion of the Roman Empire. And as it would turn out, the growing Christian empire would take inspiration from the Roman and Greek pagans by lodging accusations against their enemies regarding supposed clandestine meetings featuring infanticide, cannibalism, and incest. The image of these surreptitious gatherings can be seen as an early predecessor to the Witches' Sabbath, descriptions of which would feature the same three aforementioned acts. But there were to be several more links in the

---

6. Marcus Minucius Felix, *Octavius*, trans. Robert Ernest Wallis, in *Ante-Nicene Fathers*, vol. 4, *Tertullian*, ed. Alexander Roberts and James Donaldson (Peabody, MA: Hendrickson Publishers, 1995), 177–78.

proverbial fence, the next of which were two particular groups that had attracted the ire of the Roman Catholic Church by the start of the twelfth century. And it was their persecution that brought the Witches' Sabbath narrative one step closer to fruition.

A Poisonous Plot

On June 21, 1321, King Philip V of France issued an edict that authorized the confinement and extermination of lepers. Leprosy, an infectious disease characterized by disfiguring skin sores and nerve damage, was a major concern in France during the 1300s. The fear of contagion was palpable among people, and hysteria was widespread throughout communities. Prior to the king's edict, rumors circulated that those with leprosy had secretly been plotting to infect healthy Christians by contaminating the local wells, fountains, and rivers with poisons. On June 4, 1321, a man named Guillaume Agassa confessed to having become involved in this plot after attending a large assembly of lepers. To those present, the leader of the assembly reportedly expressed, "You see and hear how other healthy Christians hold us who are ill in shame and disrespect, and how they throw us from their meetings and gatherings and that they hold us in derision and censure and disrespect." Thus, as a form of revenge, the plot to poison Christians, to infect them with leprosy, was established. Interestingly, Agassa also mentioned that at this meeting, members were required to renounce their Christian faith. Additionally, the leader of the assembly told those in attendance that at a future gathering they would be further required to desecrate a host and trample a cross underfoot—apostatic acts that would later become a common feature of the Witches' Sabbath narrative.[7]

While in some areas it was believed that the lepers were alone in their actions, in others it was thought that there were other forces at play. For example, in one confession it was explained that the condemned had actually been paid by a Jewish individual who had given him poison to

---

7. Malcolm Barber, "Lepers, Jews and Moslems: The Plot to Overthrow Christendom in 1321," *History* 66, no. 216 (1981): 7–8.

scatter in the local water supply. Various recipes were given for that poison, including one that contained human blood, urine, three herbs, and a consecrated host—all of which were dried and reduced to a powder that was placed in small, weighted pouches. In other accounts it was the Muslim king of Granada who offered the Jewish people a great sum of money so that they would dispatch of the Christians for him. In order to avoid suspicion, though, the Jewish people contracted lepers to do the job for them.[8]

As a result of the widespread hysteria, the various conspiracy theories, and finally King Philip's edict, individuals with leprosy (including children) were incarcerated. As per Philip's orders, lepers were questioned by authorities and those who confessed to having participated in the plot were subsequently burned at the stake. The only exceptions were women who were pregnant and children under the age of fourteen. The former would be burnt only after giving birth and the latter after they had reached maturity. Anyone who refused to confess was subjected to various methods of torture until they admitted their guilt. Those who refused to comply even after being tortured were kept in prison.[9] While the king's edict said nothing about the Jewish people, there were still rampant massacres, such as one in Chinon where 160 Jews were burned alive in a large pit.[10] During the following decade, though, the fear of lepers and the resulting conspiracy theories about supposed poisonous plots rapidly dissipated. On October 31, 1338, Pope Benedict XII issued a bull in which he stated that the court had—at some point earlier—declared the lepers to be innocent of the crimes they had been accused of in previous years.[11] But the damage had already been done, and while lepers appeared to have received absolution, the same could not be said for the Jewish people.

---

8. Carlo Ginzburg, *Ecstasies: Deciphering the Witches' Sabbath*, trans. Raymond Rosenthal (New York: Pantheon Books, 1991), 35.

9. Barber, "Lepers, Jews and Moslems," 3.

10. Jeffrey Richards, *Sex, Dissidence and Damnation* (New York: Routledge, 1994), 163.

11. Ginzburg, *Ecstasies*, 53.

Unfortunately for the Jews, and other groups the Christians would come to deem heretical, the persecution was only just beginning.

Heretical Sects

Heresy, which includes any belief or practice that deviated from the Roman Catholic orthodoxy, was a relatively small concern before the twelfth century. Prior to that time, cases were generally focused on individuals or small groups instead of larger sects. However, this changed moving forward into the 1100s as dissenting groups became more organized and popular. By the year 1184 the first wave of the Medieval Inquisition, known as the *Episcopal Inquisition,* was established by Pope Lucius III for the purposes of rooting out heretics—in this case a group known as the Catharists. In 1231 another inquisition, this time known as the *Papal Inquisition,* was launched by Pope Gregory IX, in which a sect known as the Waldensians were persecuted. Of all the various groups deemed heretical, it would be the Waldensians who came to be most strongly associated with Witchcraft, and it may have been the demonization of this particular group that helped further propagate the Witches' Sabbath narrative.

Reportedly founded by a man named Valdés, the Waldensian movement emerged during the late 1170s in Lyon, France. Valdés had been a wealthy merchant who, after being moved by the story of St. Alexis, gave up his fortune and began to preach about impoverishment as a means for attaining spiritual perfection. He quickly attracted followers who were known as the "Poor of Christ" or the "Poor Men of Lyons." Like their founder, the Waldensians strived for religious purity by renouncing their material possessions and surviving solely off alms. Beyond that, though, the movement was rooted in deep disagreements with the ways in which the Roman Catholic Church was being run. Thus, adherents rejected many of the Church's entrapments, including its established hierarchy. Instead of having specifically ordained clergy, anyone within the movement who felt compelled—including women—was allowed to take on the mantle of preacher. Additionally, the Waldensians spurned the

Church's elaborate ceremonies and instead focused on a limited ortho-praxy that included simple rituals performed on a minimal basis. These rites included only three sacraments: baptism, birth, and the eucharist, the latter only being observed once a year. Not only did these beliefs and practices significantly deviate from the Church, but they also threatened its authority and its control over the Bible, which the Waldensian preach-ers had translated from Latin and disseminated among their people. Thus, by 1184 the Waldensians had unsurprisingly been denounced as heretics, and their persecution began shortly thereafter.[12]

The condemnation of heretical sects, including the Waldensians, was fueled by the same rumors that had plagued the early Christians, lepers, and Jews before them. Pope Gregory IX had lent his authority to the growing concerns when he issued a bull in 1233 known as *Vox in Rama* which condemned heresy and promoted crusades against it. More impor-tantly, the bull contained vivid imagery regarding the practices and beliefs of supposed heretical sects—including nocturnal meetings featuring acts of apostasy, Devil worship, and incestuous orgies.[13] In the year 1338, a Franciscan man by the name of John wrote about heretics, who were likely Waldensians, who were being tortured and burned at the stake in Austria and other neighboring countries. In his writing, John outlined the rituals supposedly practiced by these heretics, which included the appearance of a richly clad man who announced himself as the King of Heaven. This king, who was said to have actually been Lucifer himself, commanded the heretics to obey and expound his doctrine before extinguishing the lights and turning them over to orgiastic chaos.[14]

Due to the severity of the resulting persecution, by the fourteenth cen-tury nearly all the Waldensians—who had been most active in France and Italy—retreated up into the Western Alps. There they were able to form

---

12. Richards, *Sex, Dissidence and Damnation*, 46–47.

13. Pope Gregory IX, "Vox in Rama," in *Witchcraft in Europe: 400–1700*, ed. Alan Charles Kors and Edward Peters (Philadelphia: University of Pennsylvania, 2001), 114–16.

14. Norman Cohn, *Europe's Inner Demons*, (Chicago: University of Chicago Press, 2000), 53–54.

a stronghold that remained relatively impenetrable for some time. However, the traveling Waldensian preachers who were still active remained at risk for capture. In 1387, a man named Antonio Galosna was imprisoned for many months before finally confessing that he had attended nocturnal meetings of Waldensians. He reported that during those meetings, members ate bread and drank a special beverage made from the excrement of a toad. Attendees promised to worship a dragon who would wage war on God and his angels before they proceeded to engage in the stereotypical orgy.[15] Demonstrating the persistence of these beliefs, a century later in 1492, a Waldensian man named Martin was captured and confessed to preaching at a nocturnal synagogue. According to Martin's confession, after giving his sermon, the single candle that illuminated the meeting was extinguished and acts of sexual congress took place. Martin claimed that any children born of such unions were more apt to take on the role of preacher when grown. Interestingly, another preacher who was captured alongside Martin gave similar details regarding the nighttime congregation but added that their practices derived from the worship of an idol known variously as Bacchus, Baron, Sibyl, and the faeries.[16]

As the Waldensians continued to experience fierce persecution, a new type of crime began to develop in the imaginations of learned authorities. The crime in question was a blend of heresy and *sorcery*, or the practice of magic that involves making pacts with demons in order to acquire power. Writing in 1376, the inquisitor Nicolau Eymeric expressed his opinion that there were certain magicians who obtained their power through honoring demons and that in doing so, these practitioners were also guilty of heresy.[17] His reasoning was that, in making pacts with demons, the individual was expressing a belief in the divine power of something other than

---

15. Henry Charles Lea, *A History of the Inquisition of the Middle Ages*, vol. 2 (New York: Harper & Brothers, 1888), 257–58.

16. Thomas Hatsis, *The Witches' Ointment* (Rochester, VT: Park Street Press, 2015), 55.

17. Nicolau Eymeric, "The Directorium inquisitorum," in *Witchcraft in Europe: 400–1700*, ed. Alan Charles Kors and Edward Peters (Philadelphia: University of Pennsylvania, 2001), 120–27.

the Christian God, which was in direct opposition to the Church's teachings. Prior to the 1400s, there seems to have only been an arbitrary distinction between sorcery and those magical practices that did not involve infernal agreements. The latter, which can be labeled as *folk magic*, typically relied on the help of God or saints to achieve magical goals. However, the line that separated those two types of magical practice became increasingly blurred, and common folk magic began to be included within the broader definition of sorcery. For instance, in 1398 the theology faculty of the University of Paris—who was considered to hold the "first rank in the science of sacred letters" by the French crown—condemned "magical arts or other superstitions" alongside working with demons.[18]

As this new type of crime developed, which many modern scholars refer to as *diabolical Witchcraft*, it came to be associated specifically with the Waldensians. For example, during a series of trials held in Fribourg during the 1430s, a number of Waldensians were accused of attending heretical assemblies and having magical powers. Thus, the earlier rumors of infanticide, cannibalism, incestuous orgies, and apostasy were blended with the newer concerns regarding heresy and sorcery. Altogether, these acts formed the crime of diabolical Witchcraft, which was then grafted onto heretical sects, in particular the Waldensians. In fact, the word *Waldensian* itself (*Vaudois*, in the French-speaking Alps) even came to be used synonymously with *Witch*.[19] But while the persecution of the aforementioned groups provided a framework for emerging ecclesiastical ideas regarding the Sabbath, other more folkloric components had been developing at the same time—fantastical elements that would eventually find their way into the narrative of the Witches' Sabbath, adding to it an Otherworldly, supernatural flare.

---

18. Theology Faculty of the University of Paris, "The Theology Faculty of the University of Paris Condemns Sorcery," in *Witchcraft in Europe: 400–1700*, ed. Alan Charles Kors and Edward Peters (Philadelphia: University of Pennsylvania, 2001), 127–32.

19. Hans Peter Broedel, "Fifteenth-Century Witch Beliefs," in *The Oxford Handbook of Witchcraft in Early Modern Europe and Colonial America*, ed. Brian P. Levack (Oxford: Oxford University Press, 2013), 40–41.

The Birds That Fly by Night

In ancient Rome, the night was thought to be a haunted and perilous time. It was during those hours of darkness that frightening creatures were said to freely walk the earth. One such creature, known as the *strix* (plural form *striges* or *strigae*), was an owl-like being who was believed to have a penchant for poisoning unprotected infants before cannibalizing their bodies. Written in the year 8 CE, Ovid's *Fasti* contained references to the striges, who were described as birds with gray feathers, hooked beaks, grasping talons, and eyes nearly the size of their entire heads. These monstrous avians flew around during the night, emitting unearthly screeches as they searched for unattended babies, whom they would snatch from their cradles before ravenously consuming their entrails.[20]

However, it was held by some that the striges were not actual birds but rather bloodthirsty women who had the ability to shapeshift. In this regard, they were similar to Roman Witches, who were also believed to possess the power of metamorphosis. And thus, it was thought to be plausible that the striges were actually cannibalistic Witches who had transformed themselves into birds. In fact, by the first century CE, the term *strigae* had been defined by the grammarian Sextus Pompeius Festus as the name for women who practiced magic and flew by night.[21] Belief in the striges continued well past the classical period and spread geographically, taking root most thoroughly in the Germanic regions to the north of Rome. During the sixth century, mentions of the striges were given in the *Lex salica*—one of the earliest bodies of Germanic law. The *Lex salica*, which was written by the Frankish King Clovis, treated the striges (referred to in the text as *striae*) as a reality. The text provided the recommended punishments for those who were proven to be a strix along with those for anyone who made false accusations. However, Clovis's writing also contained a reference to

---

20. Ovid, *The Fasti of Ovid*, trans. John Benson Rose (London: Dorrell and Sons, 1866), 178–79.

21. Sextus Pompeius Festus, *De verborum significatione*, col. 1668, in *Patrologia Latina* 95 (Paris: Jacques-Paul Migne, 1861), paraphrased in Ronald Hutton, *The Witch* (New Haven: Yale University Press, 2017), 70–71.

another type of individual known as a *herburgius*, which was defined as "one who carries a cauldron to where the *striae* do their cooking."[22] Thus, the image of the striges provided in the *Lex Salicia* suggested they were not solitary in nature. Instead, they were now depicted as gathering in assemblies where they would cook children within cauldrons before devouring them in a communal-style feast—an image all too similar to later stories of Witches and their Sabbath meetings.

Stretching further into the later Middle Ages, the notion of the cannibalistic night-flying woman continued to have a lasting impact, causing great fear among the common people. Writing in the eleventh century, the German bishop Burchard of Worms discussed these nightmarish ladies in his book *Decretum*. In essence, the *Decretum* was a book that was penned with the intention of dismantling the superstitious beliefs that were held among the general populace. As such, Burchard's text provides an insightful look into the popular folklore of the time. Although he didn't refer to them specifically as striges, in chapter 19 (entitled *De paenitentia*, also referred to as the *Corrector Burchardi*), Burchard noted a belief held by the common people that certain women flew together through the night, murdering Christians before cooking and consuming their boiled flesh.[23] Given the *Decretum's* nature as a lambasting of popular superstitions, it exemplifies just how firm beliefs regarding cannibalistic night-flying women were and how far they had spread. And, as will later be demonstrated, Burchard's *Decretum* served as inspiration for many later writers on the subjects of Witchcraft and demonology. Thus, ideas regarding these terrifying, flesh-hungry women evolved substantially from the classical period to the early Middle Ages, and they were primed and ready to provide folkloric nuance to later visions of the Witches' Sabbath.

---

22. King Clovis, "Pactus Legis Salicae," in *The Laws of the Salian Franks*, ed. and trans. Katherine Fischer Drew (Philadelphia: University of Pennsylvania Press, 1991), 125.

23. Burchard of Worms, "The Corrector, sive Medicus," in *Witchcraft in Europe: 400–1700*, ed. Alan Charles Kors and Edward Peters (Philadelphia: University of Pennsylvania, 2001), 63–67.

Night-Wandering Women

As vital as they were, ghastly tales of beastly women were not the only ones that would influence the Witches' Sabbath narrative. In fact, there were other supernatural women—ones who wandered the night with relatively more beneficent intentions—who would prove just as instrumental in the Sabbath's development. As noted earlier, Burchard's *Decretum* contained further important references, including a passage from Roman Catholic law known as the *canon Episcopi*. First recorded in 906 by Regino of Prüm, the passage in question stated, "It is also not to be omitted that some wicked women, who have given themselves back to Satan and been seduced by the illusions and phantasms of demons, believe and profess that, in the hours of night, they ride upon certain beasts with Diana, the goddess of Pagans, and an innumerable multitude of women, and in the silence of the night traverse great spaces of earth, and obey her commands as of their lady, and are summoned to her service on certain nights."[24] This passage is of importance not only because of the considerable debate it would spark among persecutors and writers during the Witch Trials, but also due to the deeper folklore regarding night-wandering women that it hinted at.

In Burchard's *Decretum*, the folklore of night-wandering women was further expanded upon. Within chapter 19, alongside his question regarding belief in cannibalistic women, Burchard poses three questions pertaining to other night-wandering women. The first question concerned a belief in women who rode through the night upon beasts, alongside a horde of other women (who were noted as being demons in disguise). He adds that this throng of demonesses was led by *Hulda*, a female spirit from Germanic folklore. The second question regarded the women mentioned in the *canon Episcopi*. In fact, the bulk of this question contains a direct quotation of the specific passage relating to Diana. The third question dealt with the belief that, on certain nights of the year, food, drink, and three knives

---

24. Regino of Prüm, "A Warning to Bishops, the Canon Episcopi," in *Witchcraft in Europe: 400–1700*, ed. Alan Charles Kors and Edward Peters (Philadelphia: University of Pennsylvania, 2001), 61–62.

should be left upon the table in order to receive blessings from three visiting sisters (who he says were known in the past as the Fates).[25]

From the thirteenth century onward, stories regarding the night-wandering women continued to expand. Sometime during the 1230s, French theologian William of Auvergne wrote of "the ladies" and their leader—whom he named Satia or Abundia—and how they were said to visit the homes of humans during the night. If food and drink had been left out for them, they would feast before blessing the home. However, if no offerings had been made, they would leave behind misfortune instead.[26] In Germany, the preacher Bertold of Regensburg warned people not to give credence to nocturnal spirits, including night wanderers, blessed ladies, and those whom he referred to as *hulden* (benevolent) and *unhulden* (malevolent). It was for these spirits, he said, that many peasant women left their tables covered with food when they went to sleep at night.[27] Stretching into the late fourteenth century, French author Jean de Meun made mention of "sorcerers" who claimed to wander at night alongside Lady Abundance in his additions to the text known as *Roman de la Rose* (originally written in the 1320s by French poet Guillaume de Lorris). Additionally, these sorcerers left their physical bodies behind to travel in spirit with "good ladies."[28]

It was in the fourteenth century that the concept of the night-wandering women began to appear in trial records. The most commonly cited cases are those of two women who were tried in Milan, Italy during 1384 and 1390. On April 30, 1384, a woman named Sibillia de Fraguliati

25. Burchard of Worms, "The Corrector, sive Medicus," in *Witchcraft in Europe: 400–1700*, 63–67.

26. William of Auvergne, *De Universo*, vol. 1 (Paris: Operamania, 1674), 1,036, quoted in Claude Lecouteux, *Phantom Armies of the Night*, trans. Jon E. Graham (Rochester, VT: Inner Traditions, 2011), 14–15.

27. Johannes Agricola, *Sybenhundertundfünfftzig Teutscher Sprichwörter* (Hagenau: n.p., 1534), no. 667, quoted in Claude Lecouteux, *Phantom Armies of the Night*, trans. Jon E. Graham (Rochester, VT: Inner Traditions, 2011), 145–46.

28. Guillaume de Lorris and Jean de Meun, *Romance of the Rose*, trans. Charles Dahlberg (Princeton, NJ: Princeton University Press, 1995), 305–6.

confessed that she had attended weekly meetings held by a mysterious woman known only as Madame Oriente. The meetings took place every Thursday night and would begin with a ritual of reverence in which Sibillia and the other attendees would bow their heads and say, "Be well, Madame Oriente." Oriente would respond, "Welcome, my daughters." Six years later, a woman named Pierina de Bripio also confessed to attending the Thursday night meetings with Madame Oriente. Her confession contained many similarities to Sibillia's but provided several new details. For example, according to Pierina, the spirits of hanged and decapitated people also attended the gatherings. Madame Oriente and her followers would roam from house to house, eating and drinking. Additionally, Oriente taught her followers the uses of various herbs, how to locate stolen or lost objects, and how to undo spells.[29] Perhaps one of Madame Oriente's most impressive acts of magic, though, occurred after she and her followers had slaughtered and feasted on oxen. Oriente would arrange the bones of a butchered ox under its hide before tapping it with the pommel of a wand. Miraculously, the ox would then be brought back to life—although it was noted that, after their resurrection, these oxen were no longer able to work in the fields.[30]

The Faerie Sabbath

Just as every culture has their Witches, they also have their faeries, and the folklore regarding the two overlapped with one another considerably. Whether it was due to their similar Otherworldly powers or because they were both viewed by Christians as being agents of Satan, Witches and faeries have often gone hand in hand. During the Witch Trials, it was not uncommon for faerie-related beliefs to find their way into confessions and other writing. For instance, in *Daemonologie* (1597) King James VI of Scotland described his encounters with accused Witches who went to their deaths continuing to express a belief that they had been trans-

---

29. Hatsis, *The Witches' Ointment*, 34–36.

30. Ginzburg, *Ecstasies*, 93.

ported by faeries to a hollow hill where they met with the "faire Queene" and were given a magical stone with "sundrie vertues."[31] Within James's statement can be found one of the key crossovers between Witches and faeries: their assemblies. Both gatherings included acts of merriment such as feasting and dancing presided over by a supernatural leader—Witches being led by the Devil and faeries by their queen. But beyond just observable similarities, at times accused Witches actually confessed to having attended what could be referred to as a *Faerie Sabbath*.

Accounts of Faerie Sabbaths were quite popular in Scotland, where there was a deeply ingrained belief in the *Fair Folk* or the *Good Neighbours*, euphemisms commonly used for faeries so as not to offend them. For example, Alison Pearson of Fife confessed in 1588 to "hanting and repairing with the gude nychtbouris and Queen of Elfame." Pearson had explained to her interrogators that she had spent several years with the faeries but that she could not recall just how many. Additionally, she recounted how she had once traveled with the faeries, witnessing great merriment and cheer being made to the music of a pipe as well as wine being drunk from goblets.[32] Isobel Gowdie of Auldearn, Scotland, confessed in 1662 that she had gone to the Downie-Hills and received meat from the "Qwein of Fearrie." She described the queen as being elegantly dressed in white and brown clothes. She also mentioned a "King of Faerrie," who was a fine-looking man, being well favored and having a broad face.[33] Agnes Cairnes of Kirkcudbright, Scotland, confessed in 1659 that she had been away with the faeries, having attended a great meeting on Beltane with "the not earthen folkis" who spoke

31. James VI, *Daemonologie*, ed. G. B. Harrison (London: John Lane, 1922–26; electronic reproduction by John Bruno Hare, Internet Sacred Text Archive, accessed February 5, 2021), 75, https://www.sacred-texts.com/pag/kjd/index.htm.

32. Robert Pitcairn, *Ancient Criminal Trials in Scotland*, vol. 1 (Edinburgh: Ballantyne and Co., 1833), 163.

33. Robert Pitcairn, *Ancient Criminal Trials in Scotland*, vol. 3 (Edinburgh: Ballantyne and Co., 1833), 604.

in an "eldridge voyce." At this meeting she described there having been a fire as well as "dancing and myrth."[34]

The Faerie Sabbath was also present in Italy, particularly in Sicily during the sixteenth and seventeenth centuries. It was here that a specific folklore developed regarding the *doñas de fuera*, or the "ladies from the outside." These ladies included faeries and the human women who associated with them. In many ways, the Sicilian faerie women resembled stereotypical Witches, and the Spanish people actually used the terms *brujas* and *doñas de fuera* interchangeably. Specifically, the doñas de fuera were said to gather in groups known as companies, which were led by the *Reina de las Hadas*, or the Queen of the Faeries. Accounts of their assemblies featured many of the same characteristics as the Witches' Sabbath. For instance, an unnamed woman from Palermo in Sicily confessed in 1588 that she flew with a throng of women on billy goats to Benevento. Here there were a king and queen, the former being described as a red young man and the latter a beautiful woman. The unnamed woman explained how she was told to renounce God and Our Lady and that if she were to worship the king and queen instead, they would help her by granting wealth, beauty, and men to love her. She swore her oath upon a book and promised them her body and soul. Afterward, there was a feast followed by sexual congress.[35]

The Wild Hunt

Another piece of folklore that several modern scholars have cited as a possible point of origin for the Sabbath narrative is the Wild Hunt. The Hunt can be roughly defined as an eldritch cavalcade composed of ghosts and other spirits, including the souls of the living who had been swept up into its folds. These Otherworldly processions were nocturnal and

---

34. "Agnes (Bigis) Cairnes (5/4/1659)," Survey of Scottish Witchcraft Database, accessed February 5, 2021, http://witches.shca.ed.ac.uk/index.cfm?fuseaction=home.case record&caseref=C%2FEGD%2F792&search_type=searchaccused&search_string =lastname%3Dcairnes.

35. Gustav Henningsen, "'The Ladies from Outside': An Archaic Pattern of the Witches' Sabbath," in *Early Modern European Witchcraft*, ed. Bengt Ankarloo and Gustav Henningsen (Oxford: Claredon Press, 1990), 195–97.

variously led by a divine or semidivine leader such as Diana, Herodias, Holda, Perchte, Odin/Wotan, Herla, or Herne. Historian Carlo Ginzburg referred to this supernatural hunt when he stated that the folkloric nucleus of the Sabbath lies in the ancient theme of the living making ecstatic journeys into the realm of the dead.[36] However, like the concept of the Sabbath itself, the Wild Hunt hasn't always been a monolithic one. Instead, the term *Wild Hunt* functions more as an umbrella under which a number of folklore stories have come to fall. In fact, it appears to have been Jacob Grimm's book *Deutsche Mythologie* (first published in 1835) that was responsible for bringing many of these stories together and forming the highly codified image as described above.[37]

That being said, Grimm did pull from a variety of early and late medieval texts which may have, directly or indirectly, influenced the Sabbath narrative. In particular, he drew from folklore regarding two types of nocturnal processions and interwove them into a new, unified construct. The first is one that we have just discussed, the night-wandering women who were often led by a female spirit such as Diana, Abundia, or Satia. The second type of procession was that which consisted of spirits, namely those of people who had committed grievous sins during their life or who had died prematurely. Stories pertaining to these roaming bands of spirits grew in popularity starting in the eleventh century, particularly in response to a story given by a Anglo-Saxon monk named Ordericus Vitalis. According to Vitalis, he had been approached by a priest who described how, on New Year's Night of 1091 (or 1092 in some translations), he had witnessed a long and noisy procession of ghosts. These spirits were all being tormented in ways that matched the sins they had committed while alive. The priest noted that only masses and prayers offered by the living could shorten the suffering of these spirits and eventually set them free. He finished his story by explaining that he had

---

36. Ginzburg, *Ecstasies*, 101.

37. Jacob Grimm, *Teutonic Mythology*, trans. James Steven Stallybrass, vol. 3 (London: George Bell & Sons, 1883), 918–50.

recognized this procession as *familia Herlechini*, a name which he unfortunately did not elaborate on.[38]

By the late twelfth century, the concept of traveling packs of spirits, being tormented for their sins and seeking penitence, had become a common literary trope across England, France, and the Rhineland. These spectral groups were variously known as the Army or Retinue of Herlewin, Hellequin, or Herla.[39] Moving into the thirteenth century, ideas and beliefs regarding trooping spirits spread further into Germany, where they took root and continued to evolve. Here it became known as *das wütende Heer*, or the "Furious Army." While these stories grew to have a similar feel to our modern image of the hunt, they still lacked a distinguishable leader. However, this changed in the sixteenth century when a Protestant theologian named Johannes Agricola explained how the troop was preceded by an old man named Loyal Eckhart. This man went about commanding people to move back, suggesting that some return to their homes if they wished to avoid misfortune. A century prior, in 1497, an Italian man named Zuanne della Piatte testified that he had visited the Mountain of Venus, where he met Eckhart along with Dame Herodias.[40] Dame Herodias, who was a female spirit of biblical origin, had previously been included in Burchard's version of the *canon Episcopi* alongside Diana as the leader of a nocturnal procession of women.[41]

Thus, it all comes full circle, back to the notion of night-wandering women who were led by a female spirit. There is some evidence that these processions eventually intermingled with stories of the Furious Army. For example, a sixteenth-century woman from Bern, Germany, was exiled after

---

38. Ordericus Vitalis, *The Ecclesiastical History of England and Normandy*, trans. Thomas Forester, vol. 2 (London: H. G. Bohn, 1854), 511–20.

39. Hutton, *The Witch*, 128–30.

40. Claude Lecouteux, *Phantom Armies of the Night*, trans. Jon E. Graham (Rochester: Inner Traditions, 2011), 145–46.

41. Carlo Ginzburg, *The Night Battles: Witchcraft and Agrarian Cults in the Sixteenth and Seventeenth Centuries*, trans. John Tedeschi and Anne C. Tedeschi (Baltimore, MD: John Hopkins University Press, 2013), 90; Burchard of Worms, *Decretorum Liber Decimus*, in *Patrologiae cursus completus...*, vol. 140 (Paris: Jacques-Paul Migne, 1880), 425.

confessing that she had ridden with *Frow Selden* in the *wüttisheer* (the Furious Army).[42] Certainly, the two were melded together in Grimm's writing on the Wild Hunt. However, it is difficult to ascertain to what degree the Furious Army had influence on the development of the Witches' Sabbath narrative. It is much easier to see the direct impact processions of night-wandering women had on the Sabbath. As it has been seen, traces of stories about these women, such as those encapsulated in the *canon Episcopi*, can be found in early conceptualizations of the Sabbath. There is even one rare case in which a direct mention of such a procession found its way into a trial confession. In this case, an accused Witch from Hesse, Germany, admitted in 1630 that he had been a member in Dame Holle's retinue. He detailed how he had followed her on New Year's Day into the mountain known as Venusberg.[43]

The Council of Basel

Shortly before his death in February of 1431, Pope Martin V called for a general council of the Roman Catholic Church to be held in Basel, Switzerland. The meeting was later confirmed by his successor, Pope Eugenius IV. The primary purpose of this council was to address the weakening of the papacy caused by the Great Schism—a period of time during which there were two rival popes. However, the council was also held to address concerns regarding a heretical group known as the Hussites, followers of the religious reformer Jan Hus who had broken with Roman Catholic tradition by using Czech liturgy and administering Holy Communion to the laity in both forms (i.e., bread and wine, instead of bread alone). While there is no evidence to suggest that Witchcraft was formally discussed during the council's duration, it was almost certainly talked about informally among those in attendance. In fact, it is widely believed that the Council of Basel was the epicenter for the dissemination of beliefs regarding Witchcraft and demonology—specifically theories regarding

---

42. Lotte Motz, "The Winter Goddess: Percht, Holda, and Related Figures," *Folklore* 95, no. 2 (1984): 154.

43. Motz, "The Winter Goddess: Percht, Holda, and Related Figures," 154.

the Witches' Sabbath. Why? Because many of the individuals who were present at the Council of Basel would go on to write influential works on the topic of the Sabbath. Four texts in particular written by council attendees stand out among the rest for the substantial effects they had on furthering the Sabbath narrative, as well as their impact on the growing persecution of suspected Witches.

Formicarius by Johannes Nider

During his time at the Council of Basel, German theologian Johannes Nider collected accounts of Witchcraft that he would later cite in his *Formicarius* (The Ant Colony, a term referring to Proverbs 6:6, which claims that ant colonies represent an ideal model of discipline for humans). The text was written sometime between 1435 and 1438. The fifth book of the *Formicarius* included the confession of an unnamed man wherein he described the ceremony through which he was initiated into a sect of Witches. According to this man, the ritual took place on a Sunday in a church before the holy water had been consecrated. During the rite, he was required to renounce both Christ and his baptism before drinking an elixir made from the boiled bodies of unbaptized infants.[44]

Errores gazariorum

Written anonymously sometime in the 1430s, the *Errores gazariorum* (Errors of the Cathars, sometimes also referred to as the Errors of the Waldensians or Witches) expanded further upon the diabolical image of the heretical sect of Witches and their nocturnal meetings. Whoever the author may have been, it is known that they were working for the bishop George de Saluces, who was in attendance at the Council of Basel. The treatise described how new members of the sect were given a container of ointment and instructed on how to anoint a staff in order to fly to the synagogue. Once they arrived, the individuals were made to swear an oath of fidelity to the Devil before kissing his posterior as a sign of loyalty.

---

44. Johannes Nider, "The Formicarius," in *Witchcraft in Europe: 400–1700*, ed. Alan Charles Kors and Edward Peters (Philadelphia: University of Pennsylvania, 2001), 155–59.

Finally, the sect would engage in a feast, consuming the bodies of murdered children, before the Devil extinguished the light and an orgy ensued.[45]

Le champion des dames by Martin le Franc

Martin le Franc attended the Council of Basel, working as the secretary to Duke Amadeus VII. Later, in 1440 le Franc wrote a lengthy poem titled *Le champion des dames* (The Defender of Ladies). The poem, which is 24,384 lines long, revolves around two characters (the defender and the adversary) who debated the moral character of women. At one point within the story, the adversary described how women fly on brooms to the synagogue, where they deny Christ and kiss the Devil's posterior. At this assembly, it was also reported that there were lessons given on the art of sorcery as well as feasting, dancing, and sexual congress.[46]

Flagellum haereticorum fascinariorum by Nicolas Jacquier

Written in 1458 by the Dominican inquisitor Nicholas Jacquier, *Flagellum haereticorum fascinariorum* (Scourge of Heretical Witches) discussed further details regarding the new sect of heretical Witches. Like others to come, Jacquier was skeptical of the *canon Episcopi* and argued that the women it discussed were different from the Witches who belonged to the new sect. Jacquier argued that the women of the *canon Episcopi* were deluded and that their experiences were nothing more than dreams. He purported that sleeping people could not possibly engage in the diabolical acts of the Sabbath, citing the fact that confessed Witches often reported that after returning from the Sabbath, their bodies were exhausted. In his

45. Anonymous, "The Errores Gazariorum," in *Witchcraft in Europe: 400–1700*, ed. Alan Charles Kors and Edward Peters (Philadelphia: University of Pennsylvania, 2001), 159–62.

46. Martin le Franc, "The Defender of Ladies," in *Witchcraft in Europe: 400–1700*, ed. Alan Charles Kors and Edward Peters (Philadelphia: University of Pennsylvania, 2001), 166–69.

mind, these somatic complaints could not be caused by mere dreams and therefore proved that Witches physically went to their Sabbaths.[47]

———

Within these various written works, we can see the many disparate threads that developed over the centuries coming together to form the stereotype of the Witch and their nocturnal convocations. And by the onset of the sixteenth century, the Sabbath narrative had begun to be interjected into the growing Witch Trials. During these trials, further details were added to the Sabbath's already vivid imagery, creating striking accounts of Witches meeting with the Devil and engaging in different acts—both odious and festive. But, before diving into the fascinating layers of Sabbath accounts given in both Europe and the early American colonies, we must finish tracing the historical development of the narrative as it progressed toward the modern era.

The Sabbath in Art: *The Witches* by Hans Baldung Grien

Just as the image of the Witches' Sabbath began to take shape in the writings of learned authorities by the end of the fifteenth century, it also began to appear in various forms of art. One piece of art, which can be interpreted as depicting a Witches' Sabbath, is a woodcut by the German painter and printmaker Hans Baldung Grien. The woodcut in question, entitled *The Witches*, was completed in Strasbourg during 1510. While it is unknown if Grien meant for his woodcut to portray a Sabbath, the iconography found within it is certainly in line with the narrative of nocturnal meetings of Witches. However, what's particularly interesting about Grien's work is the fact that during the time of its creation, Witch Trials in Germany were uncommon, and texts that described Sabbath meetings had not yet been widely circulated. Thus, it would seem that Grien's

———

47. Nicholas Jacquier, "A Scourge for Heretical Witches," in *Witchcraft in Europe: 400–1700*, ed. Alan Charles Kors and Edward Peters (Philadelphia: University of Pennsylvania, 2001), 169–72.

imagery of Witches and their Sabbath may have been influenced by pre-existing folklore rather than ecclesiastical ideals.

The scene that unfolds in *The Witches* is a gloomy one, achieved through Grien's proficiency with chiaroscuro—a technique that uses light and dark shades to create strong contrast.[48] In the woodcut we see a group of Witches gathered in some desolate place. The landscape features an old, twisted tree and a ground littered with skulls, vermin, and cooking forks. Three of the Witches, who all appear rather haggard and unruly, sit in a circle around an ornate pot—calling to mind the striges mentioned in the *Lex salica*, gathering together in the night in order to cook babies within their cauldrons. One of the women in the picture has lifted the lid of the pot, releasing a dense smoke that carries what appears to be tiny frogs up into the air. Based on the presence of spoons and forks, presumably the Witches are in the process of cooking something. A fourth Witch stands behind the other three, slightly obscured but looking upward to the night sky where another Witch flies backward upon a goat. She grasps a long cooking fork, which holds a pot similar to one on the ground below. Finally, in the upper left corner, nearly lost within the thick plumes of smoke, is a sixth Witch who flies unsupported. The Witches in flight are further reminiscent of the folkloric night-wandering women, such as those described in the *canon Episcopi* and Burchard's *Decretum*.

It is tempting, from a modern perspective, to interpret these Witches as a coven who have gathered together for their Sabbath meeting. The purpose of their meeting is seemingly the creation of flying ointment—suggested by the presence of the pots, cooking tools, and assorted macabre ingredients. However, it will never be known for sure if this was Grien's intended meaning of the woodcut. Grien produced his artwork during a time when there was an increasing interest in the literature of classical Greece and Rome, which contained several Witch-type characters. That said, while it is from the mythos of the classical world that Grien

---

48. *The Witches* can be viewed online at the Met Museum website (https://www.british museum.org/collection/object/P_1895-0122-230) and the British Museum website (https://www.metmuseum.org/art/collection/search/336235).

drew his inspiration, there is one particular aspect of *The Witches* that deviates from the typical lore. Prior to the establishment of the Sabbath narrative and before its wider circulation, Witches were often believed to be independent in their malefic workings. Thus, it stands out as odd that Grien's woodcut shows a gathering of six women, which is much more aligned with later beliefs regarding retinues of Witches working together. As such, Grien's work reflects the same turning point that was happening in the minds of learned authorities regarding the nature of Witches. Whatever Grien's inspiration, and regardless of his intentions, his vision of Witches would go on to influence those created by other artists, as well as those conjured forth in the imaginations of the general population.

Chapter 2
A RESURRECTION
OF THE SABBATH

Belief in the reality of Witchcraft, and subsequently in the Sabbath itself, would greatly wane with the start of the Age of Enlightenment (1715–89). It was during this time that people began to reject their earlier superstitious beliefs in favor of intellectual and scientific reasoning. With this shift in perspective, those who had been accused and condemned as Witches in centuries prior were now seen as innocent victims rather than perpetrators of evil. The laws regarding Witchcraft and magic would change too, further reflecting the decline in superstitious belief. In Great Britain specifically, the previous laws were replaced with a new act in 1735 under which the supposed practice of Witchcraft was no longer considered a capital offense. Instead, the Witchcraft Act of 1735 focused on punishing, through fines and jail time, those who claimed to have magical powers—not because they were believed to be a legitimate supernatural threat but because they were considered con artists. However, despite the intellectual expansion brought on during the Age of Enlightenment, the mythos regarding Witches and their nocturnal Sabbaths would never fade away completely. In fact, it would only be a matter of time before the concept of the Sabbath would be resurrected through the work of various scholars, artists, and occultists. And as the Sabbath re-emerged in the modern era and into today's practice of Witchcraft, it would come to exist in ways both consistent with and also divergent from the pre-established folklore.

The Witch-Cult

As mentioned, the growing consensus during the Age of Enlightenment was that those who were persecuted during the Witch Trials had, in reality, been innocent of their alleged crimes. They were not Witches but rather innocent bystanders who were the unfortunate victims of mass hysteria. However, an alternative theory slowly emerged among certain scholars which suggested that the accused may not have been completely without guilt. Referred to today as the *Witch-Cult Hypothesis*, this theory asserted that accused Witches had actually been members of an underground cult that was itself either a continuation or a degenerate form of an ancient pagan religion. To back their claims, scholars pulled from trial transcripts, consequently helping preserve much of the folklore found therein. But while the Witch-Cult Hypothesis certainly provided a rather tantalizing version of historical events, it was eventually debunked. Today, it is generally accepted that there never was a secret yet widespread religion of Witches in Europe. Yet despite its lack of historical merit, the Witch-Cult Hypothesis would eventually have an undeniable impact on the Modern Witchcraft Revival—a period of renewed interest in Witchcraft beginning in the mid-twentieth century. During said revival, the folklore that had been retained within the Witch-Cult Hypothesis—including that regarding the Sabbath—would be taken and applied to modern practice. As such, the Witches' Sabbath would find new life among contemporary practitioners.

Today, when you hear about the Witch-Cult Hypothesis, it is most often attributed to the Egyptologist, archaeologist, anthropologist, historian, and folklorist Margaret Murray. In 1921, Murray published her seminal book, *The Witch-Cult in Western Europe*. Within the text, she provided what was arguably the most in-depth analysis of the supposed secret European religion of Witches. However, while Murray's work would prove to be most influential on modern Witchcraft, the hypothesis itself did not, in fact, originate with her. Given the amount of attention, or rather criticism, Murray has faced regarding the Witch-Cult Hypothesis, it may be surprising to learn that she had inherited it from several scholarly predecessors.

The first iteration of the Witch-Cult Hypothesis can be found in the writings of Girolamo Tartarotti, an Italian abbot and writer on the subject of Witchcraft. In 1749, Tartarotti penned a text entitled *Del Congresso Notturno delle Lammie*, in which he attempted to find the midground between superstition and skepticism regarding Witchcraft. It was within his book that Tartarotti rather boldly commented, "The witches of our time are derived from, and are the offspring of, the ancient ones, who were followers of Diana, and Erodiade, and that their crime is witchcraft, just as it was in the past."[49] His statement was extremely controversial in that by suggesting the practice of Witchcraft was a remnant of ancient paganism, Tartarotti was breaking from the Church's image of Witches being Devil-worshippers. In response, the Church admonished Tartarotti, and he was eventually forced to issue a retraction in 1751 entitled *Apologia del Congresso Notturno delle Lammie*. Despite the apology, the seeds of Tararotti's initial claims rapidly spread and would soon sprout in the minds of other like-minded individuals.

A century later, in 1828 a German professor named Karl Ernst Jarcke expanded upon the budding Witch-Cult Hypothesis. Jarcke had been tasked with editing the records of a Witch Trial from seventeenth-century German for a legal journal. For reasons unknown, the professor took it upon himself to interject his own commentary within those edits. In doing so, he proposed that Early Modern Witchcraft had actually been a permutation of a pagan religion native to Germany. He went on to explain how paganism had lingered among the common people but that it had been denounced by the upper class as being Satanism. In response, the peasantry adapted by ironically becoming literal Devil-worshippers. Jarcke's ideas went on to influence Franz Josef Mone, a German historian. In 1839, Mone published a paper entitled *Uber das Hexenwesen* in which he adopted and altered Jarcke's claims. Seeking to defend the honor of his country's past, Mone purported that the pre-Christian religion was not

---

49. Girolamo Tartarotti, *Del Congresso Notturno delle Lammie* (Venice: Libraro e Stampatore, 1749), 165, quoted in Raven Grimassi, *Old World Witchcraft* (San Francisco: Weiser Books, 2011), 50–51.

Germanic in origin but rather a foreign import. He explained that this religion was a bastardization of the classical mystery cults of Hecate and Dionysos and had been introduced by Greek slaves. In line with the early iterations of Sabbath folklore, the supposed religion focused on the worship of a goat-like god, nocturnal orgies, sorcery, and poisoning. In further defense of his homeland, Mone strongly noted this religion had been hated by both the native German pagans and the later Christians.[50]

Spreading outward from Germany, another influential person, whose ideas contributed to the re-emergence of the Witches' Sabbath, was a French historian named Jules Michelet. In 1862, Michelet published his book *La Sorcière* (later published under the title *Satanism and Witchcraft*) in which he claimed that the Witch-Cult consisted of peasants who opposed Catholicism—which he noted was the practice of the upper class. In a largely sympathetic twist, he added that Witches were mostly women who had been powerful healers. These women worshipped Pan, whom the Church had demonized and turned into their Devil.[51] Then there was the American suffragist Matilda Joslyn Gage, who wrote in her book *Woman, Church and State* (1839) about how the prehistoric world had been matriarchal and that accused Witches had really been pagan priestesses preserving the worship of a great goddess.[52] Karl Pearson, an English professor and amateur historian, furthered Gage's theory by adding that during the rise of Christianity, the cult had begun to replace the goddess with a male deity. It was this male deity who Christian persecutors eventually misconstrued as the Devil.[53] Conversely, American folklorist Charles Godfrey Leland recounted the legend of a supposed Italian Witch-Cult in his book *Aradia: Or the Gospel of the Witches* (1899). In this case the cult remained centered around the goddess Diana and her

---

50. Ronald Hutton, *Triumph of the Moon* (Oxford: Oxford University Press, 1999), 136.

51. Jules Michelet, *La Sorcière*, trans. Lionel James Trotter (London: Simpkin, Marshall, and Co., 1863), see esp. introduction.

52. Matilda Joslyn Gage, *Woman, Church and State* (New York: The Truth Seeker Company, 1893), see esp. chap. 5, "Witchcraft."

53. Hutton, *Triumph of the Moon*, 149–50.

daughter Aradia, who taught the peasantry Witchcraft so that they could punish their oppressors. According to the legend, Aradia told her followers to meet once a month upon the night of a full moon. Consistent with Sabbath lore, Aradia goes on to say, "And ye shall make the game of Benevento, extinguishing the lights, and after that shall hold your supper thus..."[54]

Thus, by the time that Murray published her book in 1921, various theories regarding a Witch-Cult had already been percolating in the minds of scholars for nearly two centuries! That being said, of the different Witch-Cult variants, it was Murray's version that was perhaps the most cohesive. At its core, Murray's Witch-Cult was a fertility religion whose members gathered together in covens in order to worship a male deity—she noted that this male deity had superseded an earlier female one. Murray differentiated between what she called *Operative Witchcraft* and *Ritual Witchcraft*. The former included the working of spells and charms, while the latter involved religious beliefs and traditions that formed the basis of the Witch-Cult.[55] According to Murray, there were two different types of meetings attended by covens of Witches, known as Sabbaths and Esbats. Breaking from traditional folklore, she provided a vague description of the Sabbath as a sort of general assembly for all those who belonged to the cult. In turn, Murray attributed all the classical elements of the Witches' Sabbath to the Esbat meetings, which she claimed were for those members who specifically carried out the cult's various ceremonies.[56]

As noted earlier, the Witch-Cult Hypothesis would ultimately be disproven by historians wholesale. But it would appear that even from its inception, the hypothesis was never taken very seriously by academics. Most scholars were in agreement that the Witch Trials had been the

54. Charles Godfrey Leland, *Aradia: Or the Gospel of the Witches* (London: Troy Books Publishing, 2018), 44–45.

55. Margaret A. Murray, *The Witch-Cult in Western Europe* (New York: Barnes and Noble, 1996), 11–12.

56. Murray, *The Witch-Cult in Western Europe*, 97–123.

result of mass hysteria and delusion, not the persecution of a clandestine pagan religion. Any contrary claims were briskly written off as sensational nonsense. For example, Michelet's *La Sorcière* was said to have been met with silence from French literary critics who had recognized it as being historically unsound.[57] It wasn't really until the twentieth century that the Witch-Cult Hypothesis gained much attention. Of course, this change was sparked by the publishing of *The Witch-Cult in Western Europe*. As it was, Murray's work became an instant lightning rod for criticism regarding the hypothesis. Among her initial critics was historian George L. Burr, who pointed out Murray's habit of erroneously assuming confessions accurately reflected the genuine experiences of suspected Witches. Additionally, he accused Murray of selectively using evidence to support her case, often normalizing supernatural occurrences in trial records or omitting them altogether in order to paint a less fantastical image of Witches.[58] Despite the validity of these critiques, it's hard to ignore the hints of misogyny contained in the voices of Murray's predominantly male detractors. The wound is further salted when considering the fact that the Witch-Cult Hypothesis's early proponents—who appear to have escaped much of the academic aspersion—were almost exclusively male. But while Murray's work was met with harsh skepticism among her academic colleagues, the Witch-Cult Hypothesis would go on to find salience in the minds of others.

Wicca, Neopaganism, and the Wheel of Year

One person who took Murray's work to heart was a retired civil servant named Gerald Brosseau Gardner. In 1951 the earlier mentioned Witchcraft Act of 1735 was finally repealed, effectively decriminalizing Witchcraft. It was in the same year that Gerald Gardner came out publicly as a practicing Witch. According to his claims, Gardner had been initiated into a surviving coven of Witches during the late 1930s. The coven, which

---

57. Hutton, *Triumph of the Moon*, 140.

58. George L. Burr, "Review of Margaret Murray's *The Witch-Cult in Western Europe*," *The American Historical Review* 27, no. 4 (1922): 780–83.

had been operating in the New Forest area of England, was purported to be akin to the very cult that Murray had pontificated upon. Gardner was said to have been given fragmentary ritual material from the Witches of the New Forest coven, which represented the remnants of the practices belonging to the Witch-Cult, which he in turn used to create the foundations of what is known today as *Wicca*. And it was within the context of the Wiccan religion that the concept of the Witches' Sabbath would grow into one of its most popular modern incarnations, the *Wheel of Year*—a set of eight seasonal ritual holidays.

During his lifetime, Gardner wrote a handful of books, including two nonfiction texts on Witchcraft and his experiences as a practitioner. In the first of these books, *Witchcraft Today* (1954), Gardner wrote, "It is, I think, fairly well known that witches observed four great festivals: May eve, August eve, November eve (Hallowe'en) and February eve. These seem to correspond to the divisions of the ancient Gaelic year by the four fire festivals of Samhaim or Samhuin (November 1), Brigid (February 1), Bealteine or Beltene (May 1) and Lughnasadh (August 1)."[59] In his second book, *The Meaning of Witchcraft* (1959), Gardner referred to the four festivals as Candlemass, May Eve, Lammas, and Halloween, adding that "the equinoxes and solstices are celebrated also, thus making the Eight Ritual Occasions, as the Witches call them." In line with Murray's two classification of Witch meetings, Gardner distinguished between the Sabbat (he seemed to have preferred the French spelling of Sabbath) and minor meetings known as Esbats. He mentioned that "traditionally, the Esbat is the meeting of the local coven for local matters, or simply for fun, and it is, or should be, held at or near the full moon."[60]

The solstices and equinoxes were celebrated along with the other Sabbats; however, they were considered "lesser" holidays. Covens would hold their rituals for these lesser Sabbats on the nearest full moon rather than on their actual date. However, in 1958 a coven in Hertfordshire wrote to

---

59. Gerald Gardner, *Witchcraft Today* (New York: Citadel Press, 2004), 130.

60. Gerald Gardner, *The Meaning of Witchcraft* (York Beach, ME: Weiser, 2004), 10.

Gardner and requested for this to change and for the solstices and equinoxes be afforded as much importance as the other four Sabbats. Gardner agreed to reverting the celebration of the solstices and equinoxes back to their actual astronomical dates. Thus, the Wheel of Year, consisting of eight Sabbat holidays, was formed. This concept would continue to evolve over the years, and in 1971 Wiccan high priest Raymond Buckland would popularize the specific names and spellings of the four greater Sabbats as Samhain, Imbolc, Beltane, and Lughnasadh in his book *Witchcraft from the Inside*.[61] Meanwhile, the solstices and equinoxes would each get their own names courtesy of an American Witch named Aidan Kelly, who chose the names Mabon (autumn equinox), Litha (summer solstice), and Ostara (spring equinox)—the winter solstice had already been referred to as Yule.[62] Today, the Wheel of Year is recognized and celebrated by more than just those who identify as Wiccans, including other Neopagan groups and even some Traditional Witches!

Each of the Wiccan Sabbats marks a change in seasonal tides, celebrating the shifting rhythms of the natural world. Additionally, these holidays follow the cyclical narrative regarding the Wiccan God and Goddess, which is mirrored in the waxing and waning energies of the sun throughout the year. Modern Wiccans commemorate the seasonal cycles and corresponding deity narrative through various rituals. While interpretations vary, in general the modern Wheel of Year and each of the Sabbats' associations therein are as follows:

Yule, around December 21

Yule, or the winter solstice, is the longest night of the year. As such, it is a time of deep introspection, when many Witches confront the metaphorical shadows both external and internal. Ritual work during this time of year often involves banishment and protection. But this is also a time of

---

61. Raymond Buckland, *Witchcraft from the Inside* (St. Paul, MN: Llewellyn Publications, 1995), 142.

62. Jason Mankey, *Witch's Wheel of Year* (Woodbury, MN: Llewellyn Publications, 2019), 32–33.

celebration, as the darkest night marks the shift toward the lengthening of sunlight in days ahead. In classical Wiccan imagery, it is at Yule that the Great Goddess gives birth to the Horned God, bringing forth the masculine, solar energy back into the world.

Imbolc, February 1

Imbolc (pronounced *IM-bulk*) is the halfway point between the winter tide and the spring tide. Many Witches celebrate Imbolc as a time of cleansing and purification. Homes and altars are cleaned in preparation for the coming spring, and rituals are performed to encourage the sun's full return. Imbolc has associations with the goddess Brigid, who was celebrated around this time by the ancient Celts. In the natural world, this is also typically the time of year when many animals, particularly sheep, begin to give birth and lactation commences. In classical Wiccan imagery, Imbolc is when the Great Goddess recovers from giving birth to the Horned God and begins to nourish him.

Ostara, around March 21

Falling on the spring equinox, Ostara (pronounced *oh-STAR-uh*) is a time of equal light and darkness. As the hours of daylight continue to increase, this is also the astronomical first day of the spring tide. Witches celebrate this Sabbat by planting seeds and setting goals for the lighter half of the year. They may also perform cleansing rituals in continued efforts to release any stagnated energy left over from the winter tide. In classical Wiccan imagery, the earth's budding is symbolic of the Horned God sprouting into a lively youth.

Beltane, May 1

Beltane (pronounced *BELL-tane*) is the height of spring tide energy, when the sun has almost regained its full strength in the sky. As a final shedding of winter's darkness, the Irish Celts would spend this day building two bonfires and driving their cattle between them—effectively purifying their livestock and protecting them from disease in the coming year.

Additionally, with the natural world bursting into blooms and the later established English traditions of May Day, the air at this time is filled with a certain romance. Modern Witches mark this Sabbat by burning large bonfires, dancing around maypoles, and celebrating love in a variety of ways. In classical Wiccan imagery, Beltane is when the Horned God, now an adult, mates with the Great Goddess. From this union, the Goddess becomes pregnant—the baby being the reincarnation of the Horned God who will be born again at Yule, effectively restarting the cycle of the Wheel of Year.

Litha, around June 21

Standing opposite Yule on the Wheel of Year, Litha (pronounced *LITH-uh*) is the longest day of the year. Astronomically being the first day of the summer tide, Litha is a time of solar celebration. It is a time of year when the Fair Folk are particularly active—an association that was popularized by William Shakespeare's beloved play *A Midsummer Night's Dream*. But while the sun's brilliant power is at its zenith, the hours of daylight start to decrease moving forward. As such, Litha celebrations often have a bittersweet edge to them, as Witches are reminded of the ephemerality of the summer tide's warmth. In classical Wiccan imagery, the sun's decreasing daily presence is mirrored in the Horned God's power, which begins to wane at this point.

Lughnasadh, August 1

Lughnasadh (pronounced *loo-NAH-saw*) is commonly thought of as being the first of three harvest holidays on the Wheel of Year, followed by Mabon and Samhain. The association with harvesting comes from the Celtic origins of this Sabbat, as this was historically the time of reaping cereal grains. Additionally, Lughnasadh is often conflated with the Christian celebration of Lammas, or Loaf Mass, which also commemorates the harvesting of grain. Today, many Witches perform rituals around harvesting both literal and metaphorical crops (such as goals achieved and wishes made manifest). It is also typical for Witches to spend this day baking bread, often in the form of a man that personifies the harvest. In classical Wiccan imagery, the start of the harvest season is tied to the Horned God, who, in his declining strength, begins to sacrifice himself in order to provide abundance to the people.

Mabon, around September 21

Being the second harvest holiday on the Wheel of Year, Mabon (pronounced *MAY-bon*) concerns the harvesting of fruits such as apples and grapes. While Lughnasadh and Samhain are considered harvest holidays, Wiccan high priest Jason Mankey points out that Mabon is often considered *the* harvest holiday.[63] Many Witches celebrate this Sabbat by giving thanks for all the blessings they have received during the past seasonal tides. As the equinox also brings equal hours of day and night, Mabon brings balance and equilibrium. Therefore, rituals can also be performed in order to banish any unwanted or negative elements from one's life. In classical Wiccan imagery, the Horned God continues to diminish in power and prepares for his final sacrifice, which will come at Samhain.

Samhain, October 31

Samhain (pronounced *SOW-in*, *sow* rhymes with *cow*) is the third and final harvest. It is a time of death and decay, as the plants wither and animals are hunted to provide food for the winter. Samhain night is often said to be when the veil between this world and next is thinnest. Thus, it is the one night a year when the spirits of the dead are believed to have an easy passage back into the mortal realm. Modern Witches and Pagans celebrate this Sabbat by honoring their ancestors and other assorted beloved dead. Samhain is also a common time for rituals of divination, allowing one to have a peek at what the future might have in store. Following classical Wiccan imagery, this is also the time when the Horned God enters the burial mound after his death, which occurs during this final reaping.

---

63. Mankey, *Witch's Wheel of Year*, 293.

An Alternative Sabbath Revival

While the Witches' Sabbath found new footing through the Witch-Cult Hypothesis and later the Wiccan religion, it also took root among occultists during the late nineteenth century and onward. But instead of assuming the guise of a fertility-based set of seasonal celebrations, the Sabbath as encountered by these occult writers was viewed as a means of accessing currents of primal power in order to initiate transformation and achieve mystical gnosis. The theories and practices of these occultists would go on to directly influence the way in which the Sabbath is approached by modern practitioners of Traditional Witchcraft. The four most prominent of these occultists were Austin Osman Spare, Kenneth and Steffi Grant, and Andrew Chumbley—with each one finding inspiration from their predecessors and extrapolating their own unique visions of the Witches' Sabbath.

Austin Osman Spare

Austin Osman Spare was born in Snow Hill in London during 1886 and grew up to become both a painter and an occultist. Spare's journey into the occult began while he was young, perhaps stemming from an early experience he had while attending St. Agnes School. According to Spare, it was during this time that he met an old fortune-teller named Mrs. Patterson who was also known as "The Witch Patterson." Mrs. Patterson claimed that she had directly descended from a long line of Witches who had managed to survive the persecution in Salem, Massachusetts. As a Witch, she was said to possess the power to tell the future, conjure images, and change her appearance at will. Spare claimed that Mrs. Patterson eventually "seduced" him and initiated him as a Witch. Whether or not this story is true, it became a central part of Spare's personal mythos.

While attending college, Spare's interest in the occult was furthered through his readings of prominent writers on the subject such as Madame Blavatsky, Cornelius Agrippa, and Éliphas Lévi. At some point (possibly in 1908), Spare met the infamous magician Aleister Crowley. Spare joined Crowley's magical group Argenteum Astrum (the Order of the Silver Star) on a probationary basis in 1909. However, he never became a full member and grew to dislike Crowley, who was rumored to have made unwanted sexual advances toward Spare.[64] In 1913 Spare published his book *The Book of Pleasure (Self-Love): The Psychology of Ecstasy*, in which he explored the subject of ecstasy, the power of the unconscious mind, and the use of sigils. Spare's use of sigils, specifically his own system known as the *alphabet of desire*, became one of his most enduring trademarks. He believed that sigils could unlock the powers of the subconscious, which could then be used to attract one's desires. Two other central themes within Spare's personal theology were the concepts of *Zos* and *Kia* (Spare's magical tradition would later be named the Zos-Kia Cultus). The former referred to the human body and mundane mind while the latter represented a sort of universal consciousness. Through various transcendental methods, the Zos could be united with Kia, which would subsequently produce higher states of consciousness.

Spare's ideas and beliefs regarding the Witches' Sabbath developed later in his life and were deviant from those being espoused by the eminent voices of the Modern Witchcraft Revival. In August of 1954, Gerald Gardner sent one of his high priestesses, Doreen Valiente, to inquire about Spare's magical services as a talismanic artist. A letter Spare wrote after his visit with Valiente sheds light on the disparities between his vision of the Sabbath and Gardner's. In the letter, and typical of Spare's latent misogyny, he described Valiente, who had used the false name of Diana Walden, as a "myopic stalky nymph." He went on to dismissively point out that "she believed the 'Witches' Sabbath was a sort of Folk dance of pretty young things."[65] Spare was formally introduced to Gerald Gardner a month later, and it was noted that the two did not get along. During their meeting, the men engaged in a heated argument over the true nature

---

64. Phil Baker, *Austin Osman Spare* (Berkeley, CA: North Atlantic Books, 2014), 59.

65. Philip Heselton, *Doreen Valiente: Witch* (Woodbury, MN: Llewellyn Publications, 2016), 89–90.

of the Witches' Sabbath. Spare would later write that he did not believe Gardner had ever met a real Witch or attended an actual Sabbath.[66]

Spare's specific ideas and beliefs about the Sabbath were reflected in one of his manuscripts entitled the *Zoëtic Grimoire of Zos*. In it he wrote that, "The Sabbath is an inverse-reversion for self-seduction; an undoing for a divertive connection: sex is used as the medium and the technique."[67] In other words, Spare viewed the Witches' Sabbath as a magical act that tapped into the powers of sexual energy in order to manifest one's desires. Spare's experiences of the Sabbath were often described as dreamlike and liminal. For instance, in a rather dramatic story, Spare recalled how he once boarded a double-decker bus late one night that was packed with women who each possessed an uncanny aura. These women appeared to have an "intense though oblique interest…in him, as if inviting him to some secret and unhallowed gathering."[68] Spare came to the realization that these women were all Witches and on their way to a Sabbath meeting—quite the modern twist! He would later describe this experience as a moment of two different dimensions colliding. The concept of the Sabbath being a place of sexual power existing in dreams and liminal spaces would continue to develop moving forward.

Kenneth and Steffi Grant

Spare's beliefs regarding the Sabbath were largely influenced by his friendship with a married couple named Kenneth and Steffi Grant. Similar to Spare, Kenneth—who was an English ceremonial magician—spent his early years reading the works of prominent occultists such as Blavatsky. In 1944, when he was twenty years old, Kenneth met Aleister Crowley and they quickly formed a working relationship. It was agreed upon that Kenneth would serve as Crowley's secretary in exchange for magical tutoring. In 1945 he was formally initiated into the Ordo Templi Orientis (OTO)

---

66. Baker, *Austin Osman Spare*, 245–46.
67. Austin Osman Spare, "Zoëtic Grimoire of Zos," in *Zos Speaks!*, ed. Kenneth Grant and Steffi Grant (London: Fulger Limited, 1998), 219.
68. Baker, *Austin Osman Spare*, 243.

and a year later into Argenteum Astrum—both occult groups associated with Crowley. He was eventually given a charter to start his own lodge, or group, within the OTO, which he named the New Isis Lodge. The lodge became active in April 1955, but Kenneth was given a letter of expulsion just three months later by Karl Germer, Crowley's successor as head of the OTO. However, Grant did not cease the activities of his lodge, which he rebelliously continued to operate for another seven years.

Kenneth married Steffi in 1948, and it was actually she who first met Austin Osman Spare. Steffi had read an article on Spare in *The Leader* and, finding herself fascinated by his character, wrote him a letter. In the spring of 1949 she visited Spare at his home, where she was shown his various works of art. Steffi was so impressed that she immediately bought a few pieces to give to Kenneth for his birthday. Steffi would later introduce Spare to Kenneth. From there, the couple formed a close bond with Spare and helped inspire his work. In fact, it was Kenneth who gave Spare his magical name, Zos vel Thanatos. Encouraged by the Grants, Spare produced a variety of manuscripts, including the aforementioned *Zoëtic Grimoire of Zos*.

Kenneth's views of the Witches' Sabbath were similar to Spare's, albeit more fleshed out—at least in written form. His ideas regarding the Sabbath are best recorded in one of his and Steffi's manuscripts (known collectively at the *Carfax Monographs*) entitled *Vinum Sabbati* (1961). Within the document, Grant wrote that "most medieval Sabbatic symbolism has reference to the astral plane where the transformations so frequently described in the literature of witchcraft were actually enacted."[69] Transformation occurred through *atavistic resurgence*—a concept previously espoused by Spare in which one follows a psychomagical path leading backward into the depths of time, effectively merging with the universal consciousness. Touching upon the early theories that the Sabbath was an inverse of the Christian religion, Grant explained how the

---

69. Kenneth Grant and Steffi Grant, *Hidden Lore: The Carfax Monographs* (London: Skoob Books Publishing, 1989), 24.

magical process of atavistic resurgence was mirrored in the reverse symbolism common in descriptions of the Witches' gatherings such as prayers
chanted backward and the dances performed counter-clockwise. He elaborated that these symbols "all are instances of reversal and symbolic of
Will and Desire turning within and down to subconscious regions, to the
remote past, there to surprise the required atavism or energy for purposes
of transformation, healing, initiation, construction or destruction."[70]

Andrew Chumbley

Picking up where Spare and the Grants left off was the work of English
magician Andrew Chumbley, eventual founder of the tradition known as
Sabbatic Craft. Not much is known about Chumbley, as he was a highly
private person and revealed little personal information to the public. He
was born on September 15, 1967, and grew up in Writtle—an English
village near Chelmsford in Essex. He seems to have had a close relationship with his parents and remained living in their home until the age of
thirty-three. Chumbley was subjected to bullying in his younger years due
to severe eczema, and it's been reported that he began experimenting with
magic as a way of getting back at his tormentors. While still in his teens,
Chumbley began working on his first book, and what would become his
magnum opus, *Azoëtia: The Grimoire of the Sabbatic Craft*. This book,
which contained the beliefs and practices of Chumbley's emerging tradition, was completed and published in 1992. It has been noted that Chumbley was inspired by Austin Osman Spare and that during the 1990s,
he operated a magical lodge that had affiliations with Kenneth Grant's
Typhonian OTO group. Additionally, Chumbley's tradition was greatly
influenced by other magical systems, including Sufism, left-hand tantra,
Thelema, Voudon, Yezidism, Gnosticism, and Arabic magic, as well as
Aztec, Sumerian, and Egyptian mythology.

The Sabbatic Craft, as Chumbley described it, "is a name for a name-
less faith. It is a term used to describe an ongoing tradition of sorcerous

---

70. Grant and Grant, *Hidden Lore: The Carfax Monographs*, 24–26.

wisdom, an initiatory path proceeding from both immediate vision and historical succession. In a historical sense, the Sabbatic Craft is usually set against the background of both rural folk magic, the so-called Cunning Craft, and the learned practise of European high ritual magic."[71] The foundation of the Sabbatic Craft was built upon what Chumbley referred to as *transcendental sorcery*, or the syncretic combination of practical spellcraft and a mystical search for gnosis. Chumbley eventually formed his own working group based around his Sabbatic Craft tradition. The group, which is still operating today, is known as the *Cultus Sabbati* and is initiatory in nature, meaning that membership can only be attained through an initiatory ritual. Additionally, membership to the group is offered by invitation only. These invitations are based on the group's observance of signs and portents. Anyone allowed admittance into the Cultus is first brought into the group's outer court, which is known as the Companie of the Serpent Cross. From there, the individual may eventually be deemed fit to join the inner court of the Cultus. The Cultus Sabbati is headed by a leader known as the Magister. Other positions in the hierarchy of the Cultus include Elder, Maid, Priest, Priestess, Summoner, Seeress, Verdelet, Chronicler, and Ward.

At the center of Chumbley's tradition is the imagery of the Witches' Sabbath, which he described as "an astral or dream convocation of magical ritualists' souls, animal selves, and a vast array of spirits, faeries and Otherworldly beings." The Sabbath is seen as existing at the "crossroads of waking, sleeping and mundane dreaming."[72] Therefore, a central practice within the Sabbatic Craft is the purposeful induction of dreamlike states that allow the practitioner access to the Sabbath and subsequent gnosis—which is often interpreted in the same manner one would interpret their mundane dreams. According to Chumbley, when approached through the practice of dreaming, it is possible for the imagery of the Sabbath to "yield new wisdom and serve as wholly apposite cyphers for the teachings

71. Andrew Chumbley, "Cultus Sabbati: Provenance, Dream, and Magistry," in *Opuscula Magica*, vol. 2, ed. Daniel A. Schulke (Richmond Vista, CA: Three Hands Press, 2011), 97.

72. Chumbley, "Cultus Sabbati: Provenance, Dream, and Magistry," 98.

of oneiric flight, atavistic transformation, wortcunning, divination, ritual-isation, dual observance, spirit-worship, and so forth."[73] In other words, engaging with the Sabbath provides not only mystical gnosis and higher states of spiritual understanding, but also lessons on the very founda-tional practices that compose the art of Witchcraft.

The Sabbath in Traditional Witchcraft

Just as the concept of the Witches' Sabbath was reinterpreted and woven into the fabric of the modern Wiccan religion, it has also become a central feature within Traditional Witchcraft. However, while the Sabbath has become a set of seasonal holidays for Wiccans, for Traditional Witches it remains an Otherworldly spirit gathering. Much of the inspiration under-lying this second modern interpretation of the Sabbath comes from the works of Spare, the Grants, and Chumbley. As such, Traditional Witches recognize the Sabbath as being a liminal, dreamlike experience much in the same way that it was described by Spare. Additionally, similar to Ken-neth Grant's explanations of atavistic resurgence, Traditional Witches view the Sabbath as a place of primordial power encoded within certain symbolism such as the backward imagery found therein. Finally, in line with Chumbley's ideas, Traditional Witches experience the Sabbath as a place of mystical gnosis and transformation. It is a place where spirit com-munication occurs and profound acts of magic can be wrought. Of course, beyond the work of these occultists, Traditional Witches draw inspiration from the folklore regarding the Sabbath, particularly that which comes from trial records. Folkloric accounts of the Witches' Sabbath are care-fully examined by practitioners in hopes of discovering secret wisdoms hidden within their imagery—wisdom that can then be extracted and used in modern practice.

However, while the written lore can provide valuable insights, it is in the direct experience of the Witches' Sabbath and the primal, atavistic current therein that true knowledge and understanding of this legendary

---

73. Chumbley, "Cultus Sabbati: Provenance, Dream, and Magistry," 100.

gathering can be attained. But in order to visit the Sabbath, Traditional Witches must first become versed in the art of *spirit flight*—the process through which the spirit leaves the physical body and enters into the Otherworld. As stated in the teachings of the Sabbatic Craft, the Sabbath is only accessible through trance and dream states in which the spirit can be lifted from the body and sent forth into the Otherworld. Therefore, in Traditional Witchcraft, practitioners lean into their powers of liminality and learn to cross the metaphorical hedge that separates our mundane world from that of spirit. It is once the practitioner arrives in this realm of spirit that their journey to the Sabbath commences, navigating through spectral landscapes, soaring across darkened skies just as our folkloric forebears did so long ago. But first, in preparation for later journeys to the Sabbath, we must take a closer look at the folklore regarding its particular location and timing as well as the specific methods allegedly used by Witches in order to get there.

Chapter 3
SABBATH HAUNTS,
TIMES, AND TRAVELS

By the onset of the Witch Trials in Europe (fifteenth century), the foundation of the Sabbath narrative had firmly solidified and its concept began to creep into the imaginations of the wider public. It was during this time, as accusations were made and trials held, that more specific details regarding the Sabbath started to emerge, adding new layers to the general framework previously established. Thus, colorful new stories about Witches and their nighttime rendezvous were generated, arising from the bones of the old mythos. These stories were often told by the common people, notably those who had been accused of Witchcraft via their confessional statements, rather than the learned authorities who had propagated the narrative in the first place. Within their stories we find ideas and beliefs about the Sabbath that are commonplace along with others that are highly idiosyncratic—not only being reflective of the specific period and region in which they were given but also of the individual imagination of their creator. And so, as we continue with our examination of the Witches' Sabbath, we must now look toward the specific folklore that has emerged over time—in particular those details relating to the location, timing, and transportation to the Sabbath ground.

Location of the Sabbath

Within the trial accounts and later assorted folklore, the different locations given for the Witches' Sabbath were incredibly diverse and wide-ranging. That said, it was most common for the Sabbath to take place somewhere outdoors. Many times, gatherings were held in a wild or desolate place where the Witches could enjoy a secured sense of privacy. It was away from prying eyes that Witches could engage in their sorcerous rituals and celebrations without fear of being discovered and punished. Additionally, many of these outdoor locations had a liminal quality to them, existing as a sort of in-between place where the human world and the spirit world collided. In this sense, specific places may have been chosen for the Sabbath due to their Otherworldly nature as well as their seclusion.

Perhaps two of the most popular destinations for the Sabbath were mountains and hills, both of which featured in countless trial confessions across different geographical locations. In Slavic regions, such as Poland and Russia, Witches were believed to meet atop Bald Mountain—a term which was used generically to describe several different mountains or hills upon which little to no plant life grew. Polish Witches were said to meet atop Łysa Góra (literally meaning Bald Mountain), a hill in the Świętokrzyskie Mountains. Witches from central France were thought to gather at the top of a mountain lava dome known as Puy-de-Dôme. An accused Frenchwoman named Jeanne Boisdeau confessed in 1594 that she rode her broomstick on the winds of the night to the summit of Puy-de-Dôme, where she gathered in a large circle with other Witches.[74] In German folklore, Sabbaths were purported to be held on the Blocksberg (known today as the Brocken), the highest peak in the Harz Mountains.

Other popular outdoor locations for the Sabbath included open areas such as meadows and fields. Accused Swedish Witches confessed to attending their Sabbaths at a place known as Blåkulla (modern spelling),

---

74. Elizabeth Pepper and John Wilcock, *Magical and Mystical Sites: Europe and the British Isles* (Grand Rapids, MI: Phanes Press, 2000), 169.

which was described as being a large meadow, the ends of which no one could see.[75] On the Spanish side of the Basque region, the Sabbath was referred to as the *akelarre* (*aquelarre* in Castilian Spanish), which translates to meadow (*larre*) of the billy goat (*aker*) and thus suggested a link to meetings in those regions having traditionally taken place in expansive grassy areas.[76] In a similar vein, three accused Witches from Guernsey—Collette Du Mont, Marie Becquet, and Isabel Becquet—confessed in 1617 that they had assembled together with the Devil upon an open stretch of seashore.[77] Meanwhile, other Witches gathered in places with more natural covering, such as those of Italian folklore who were said to congregate under the branches of a certain walnut tree in the town of Benevento.[78] Likewise, Mary Green of Somerset, England, confessed in 1665 that she and her coven of Witches met in the forest at a spot known as "Hussey's Knap."[79]

Despite a seemingly necessary need for privacy, there were also odd accounts of Sabbath meetings taking place in public spaces within local villages, towns, or cities. In these cases you're left to wonder just how, even in the dead of night, congregating Witches went unnoticed. A particularly bold example of such a public Sabbath comes from Salem, Massachusetts, where Abigail Hobbes confessed in 1692 that the meeting she attended had been conducted in the Reverend Samuel Parris's very own pasture![80] Most commonly, though, the locations of public Sabbaths

75. Anthony Horneck, "An Account of What Happened in the Kingdom of Sweden in the Years 1669, and 1670," in Joseph Glanvill, *Saducismus Triumphatus: Or, Full and Plain Evidence Concerning Witches and Apparitions* (London: S. Lownds, 1681), 321.

76. *Etymological Dictionary of Basque*, comp. R. L. Trask (Brighton, England: University of Sussex, 2008), s.v. "akelarre (*n*.)."

77. "The Confessions of Witches in Guernsey, 1617," in *The Witchcraft Sourcebook*, ed. Brian P. Levack (London: Routledge, 2015), 209–13.

78. Judika Illes, *The Element Encyclopedia of Witchcraft*, (London: HarperCollins Publishers, 2005), 665–66.

79. Joseph Glanvill, *Saducismus Triumphatus: Or, Full and Plain Evidence Concerning Witches and Apparitions* (London: S. Lownds, 1681), 163.

80. Bryan F. Le Beau, *The Story of the Salem Witch Trials* (New York: Routledge, 2016), 97.

included churchyards and the crossroads of public squares. For instance, Helen Guthrie of Scotland confessed in 1661 that her coven had gathered in the churchyard at Forfar.[81] Accused Frenchman Isaac de Queyran confessed in 1609 that he had been to Sabbaths that took place at the crossroads, and others that were hosted in public squares in front of churches. In regard to the latter, de Queyran mentioned that the Devil always erected his throne directly across from the church's high altar.[82] Additionally, two accused Witches from Burgundy, France—Antoine Tornier and Jacquema Paget—admitted to attending a Sabbath held in the courtyard of a local priory.[83]

Although outdoor spaces seemed to have been the preference for Sabbaths, they were not limited to such locations, and there exist several references to Witches coming together indoors. In these instances, the Sabbath was typically held within a private house—either one belonging to a coven member or that of an unsuspecting individual. Gonin Depertyt, a man from Corsier, Switzerland, confessed in 1606 that he had been led into the house of another Witch, wherein a meeting with the Devil occurred.[84] Demonstrating a certain amount of bravado, some Witches would even gather for their Sabbaths inside public buildings. Rather ironically, this sometimes included churches themselves. For example, Agnes Sampson of Scotland confessed in 1590 that her coven met inside the church at North Berwick. She even went on to describe how the church had been lit with black candles and how the Devil spoke down to the Witches from his perch up in the pulpit.[85]

---

81. George Ritchie Kinloch, *Reliquiae Antiquae Scoticae* (Edinburgh: Thomas G. Stevenson, 1848), 120.

82. Pierre de Lancre, *On the Inconstancy of Witches*, trans. Harriet Stone and Gerhild Scholz Williams (Tempe: Arizona Center for Medieval and Renaissance Studies, 2006), 93.

83. Henry Boguet, *An Examen of Witches* (Mineola, NY: Dover Publications, 2009), 54.

84. E. William Monter, *Witchcraft in France and Switzerland* (Ithaca, NY: Cornell University Press, 1976), 96.

85. Pitcairn, *Ancient Criminal Trials in Scotland*, vol. 1, 239.

Time of the Sabbath

The Sabbath was almost exclusively held at night, often between the hours of nightfall and dawn. Midnight was a frequently cited time for the Sabbath, perhaps for its liminal quality (being the hour between night and day). For example, in Salem, Mary Warren claimed George Burroughs blew into a trumpet at midnight in order to summon other Witches to the meeting in Samuel Parris's pasture.[86] Regardless of the specific hour, the night has long been believed to be the time when Witches and demons were most active. Daytime, on the other hand, was viewed as being intrinsically holy, as it was thought to be symbolic of God's light. For this reason, French jurist Henry Boguet wrote in his 1602 book *Discours exécrable des sorciers* that "it is no new or strange matter that Satan should hold his assemblies by night; for Jesus Christ tells us that the evildoer hates the light."[87] However, there were also rare instances in which individuals confessed to attending daytime Sabbaths. For instance, Catharine de Nagiulle of Ustaritz, France, confessed that she had gone to the Sabbath at noon after falling asleep in church and being whisked away by the Devil.[88] Of course, Boguet also pointed out a more practical reason for Witches choosing nighttime hours for their meetings—that under the cloak of darkness they were less likely to be recognized by others and thus able to openly carry out their malefic deeds without the risk of being discovered.[89]

The duration of the Sabbath varied as well, with some meetings being held at length while others were quite brief. Two cases from Switzerland provide evidence for the latter, one being a rather humorous account from Gonin Depertyt who commented on how the Devil rushed the Witches through their Sabbath meal, urging them to eat quickly because he could

---

86. "SWP No. 022: George Burroughs Executed, August 19, 1692," Salem Witch Trials Documentary Archive and Transcription Project, accessed February 5, 2021, http://salem.lib.virginia.edu/n22.html.

87. Boguet, *An Examen of Witches*, 51.

88. De Lancre, *On the Inconstancy of Witches*, 90.

89. Boguet, *An Examen of Witches*, 52.

not stay long.[90] The second case comes from the confession of a woman named Pernon Debrot who claimed to have attended a Sabbath that lasted for only an hour, from 10 to 11 p.m.[91] More commonly, though, the Sabbath was thought to be an all-night affair. A popular belief was that the festivities would only come to an end with the arrival of dawn, which was heralded by the crowing of a cock. Antoine Tornier and Jacquema Paget, along with another accused woman named Clauda Jamguillaume, confessed that they were unable to spend much time at the Sabbath because a cock crowed as soon as they had arrived and the assembly was instantly dispersed.[92]

Date of the Sabbath

As for the date of the Sabbath, it was frequently discussed in terms of happening upon a particular day of the week. As mentioned in chapter 1, Jean Bodin suggested that Saturday was a particularly auspicious night for evil spirits. Meanwhile, Pierre de Lancre noted in his 1612 book *Tableau de l'inconstance des mauvais anges et démons* that the Devil desired to put himself before the worship of all others and in doing so made Thursday his chosen day for the Sabbath (he explained that the Turks worshipped on Friday, Jews on Saturday, and Christians on Sunday).[93] Overall there appeared to be little consensus on one particular day of the week being associated with the Sabbath more so than others. Touching on this fact, Henry Boguet wrote, "I have concluded that there is no fixed day for the Sabbat, but that witches go to it whenever they are so commanded by Satan."[94] Furthermore, Sabbaths were not always limited to being held once a week. De Lancre commented that there were people who attended the Sabbath on "practically all nights."[95] Yet others confessed to attend-

---

90. Monter, *Witchcraft in France and Switzerland*, 96.

91. Monter, *Witchcraft in France and Switzerland*, 94.

92. Boguet, *An Examen of Witches*, 52.

93. De Lancre, *On the Inconstancy of Witches*, 90.

94. Boguet, *An Examen of Witches*, 53.

95. De Lancre, *On the Inconstancy of Witches*, 90.

ing the Sabbath on a biweekly or even monthly basis. For example, an unnamed woman from Eichstätt, Germany, confessed in 1637 that she went to the Sabbath twice a month, twenty-four times in a year.[96] In Italy, a woman named Vicencia la Rosa confessed in 1630 that she visited the Sabbath an astonishing three times a week![97]

While particular days of the week were mentioned in connection with the Witches' Sabbath, there were also specific holidays or festivals that were associated with it as well. Impressively providing four days of significance, Issobell Smyth of Forfar, Scotland, confessed in 1661 that her coven met for their Sabbaths on "Candlemas, Rudday, Lambemas, and Hallomas."[98] These dates were echoed by Isobel Gowdie, who confessed that her coven met quarterly.[99] Of course, these are the same dates that would later become the four major Sabbats of the modern Wheel of Year—Candlemas/Imbolc, Rudday/Beltane, Lambemas/Lughnasadh, and Hallomas/Samhain. Other important days included Midsummer, on which night Jeanne Boisdeau confessed to having gathered with her fellow Witches atop Puy-de-Dôme.[100] Within the confession of Englishwoman Margaret Johnson, made in 1633, there is mention of a Witches' meeting that took place upon All Saints' Day.[101] And Rebecca Greensmith of Hartford, Connecticut, confessed in 1663 that she planned to sign a covenant with the Devil at a "merry meeting" that was to take place on Christmas.[102]

In popular folklore, additional dates that were traditionally held as sacred by Christians paradoxically came to be associated with the Witches' Sabbath as well. For instance, Witches from Germany were believed to

---

96. "The Witch-Hunt at Eichstätt," in *The Witchcraft Sourcebook*, ed. Brian P. Levack (London: Routledge, 2015), 223.

97. Henningsen, "'The Ladies from Outside,'" in *Early Modern European Witchcraft*, 198.

98. Kinloch, *Reliquiae Antiquae Scoticae*, 133.

99. Pitcairn, *Ancient Criminal Trials in Scotland*, vol. 3, 606.

100. Pepper and Wilcock, *Magical and Mystical Sites: Europe and the British Isles*, 169.

101. John Harland and Thomas Turner Wilkinson, *Lancashire Folk-Lore* (London: Frederick Warne and Co., 1867).

102. Richard S. Ross III, *Before Salem: Witch Hunting in the Connecticut River Valley, 1647–1663* (Jefferson, NC: McFarland & Company, 2017), 256.

gather on Walpurgisnacht (April 30–May 1), the night before the feast day of Saint Walpurga, who was often invoked for protection against the powers of Witchcraft. In Russia, Witches were said to be particularly active on the night of Ivan Kupala, a celebration of the summer solstice and later identified with Saint John the Baptist. Swedish folklore held that Witches would fly off to their Sabbath at Blåkulla on the night of Maundy Thursday (the Thursday before Easter, commemorating the Last Supper). A rather amusing Swedish custom recorded by Sir William A. Craigie involved individuals hiding various implements, including oven spades and besoms, during Easter week in order to prevent Witches from traveling to the Sabbath.[103]

Transportation

Whether it was by flying on some object, such as a broomstick, or by walking on foot, the means of travel taken by Witches to their Sabbaths were highly varied. Within trial records and later folklore, both supernatural and mundane methods of transport were commonly cited—often chosen on the basis of proximity between the Sabbath location and the home of the Witch in question. For example, Isaac de Queyran explained how Witches who lived far away were transported through the air to the place where the Sabbath was being held. Meanwhile, Witches like himself, who lived nearby, simply walked to the meeting.[104] Similarly, Helen Guthrie mentioned that she and two other Witches—Isobell Shyrie and Elspet Alexander—had met together at an alehouse before heading to the Sabbath on foot.[105] Still, there were other Witches who were said to have arrived at the Sabbath on horseback. Such was the case for Agnes Sampson, who confessed to riding a horse with her son-in-law to a gathering held in the local churchyard.[106] There were even accused Witches, like a woman from Poland named Jadwiga, who claimed that they had

---

103. William A. Craigie, *Scandinavian Folk-Lore: Illustrations of the Traditional Beliefs of the Northern Peoples* (London: Alexander Gardner, 1896), 373–74.

104. De Lancre, *On the Inconstancy of Witches*, 164.

105. Kinloch, *Reliquiae Antiquae Scoticae*, 122.

106. Pitcairn, *Ancient Criminal Trials in Scotland*, vol. 1, 239.

taken carriages to the Sabbath.[107] However, these commonplace methods of transport were often completely overshadowed by the overly abundant stories about Witches taking flight and traversing the night sky in order to reach their destination.

Although it was popularly mentioned in confessional statements given by the accused, writers on the subject of Witchcraft often debated the specific nature of flight—including whether or not it was even possible. Opinions differed on whether a Witch's ability to fly was merely a delusion or if it was based in actual reality. In regard to the latter, it was debated even further on whether said flight occurred physically or in spirit form. Thus, Pierre de Lancre stated that "the question of whether the witches' travel to the sabbath is a marvel, a dream, or a satanic illusion, and whether they really go there in body or merely in spirit, has preoccupied scholars of ancient and modern times as well as the sovereign judges of the courts of parliament."[108] Oddly enough, the possibility of physical flight appears to have been supported by many writers who backed their ideas by citing biblical references regarding the different powers possessed by both God and the Devil. For example, when defending physical flight, Bodin mentioned a Gospel story in which Satan transported Jesus to the top of a temple and then onto a mountain. He explained that "it would be mocking the Gospel story to call into doubt whether the Devil transports witches from one spot to another."[109] Henry Boguet dismissed the notion of spirit flight by explaining how the soul could not be separated from the body without the individual dying. In order for the Witch to return to their body, they would need to be resurrected—a miracle which, according to the Bible, only God could perform.[110]

However, the denial of spirit flight stood in the face of the ample number of confessions given by accused Witches, which tended to include

---

107. Wanda Wyporska, *Witchcraft in Early Modern Poland 1500–1800* (New York: Palgrave Macmillan, 2013), 39.

108. De Lancre, *On the Inconstancy of Witches*, 104.

109. Bodin, *On the Demon-Mania of Witches*, 121.

110. Boguet, *An Examen of Witches*, 48–49.

accounts of both physical and spectral travel. For example, an Italian woman named Margherita of San Rocco explained in 1571 that "the visits to the games [Sabbaths] which I have made did not take place in person, but in spirit, leaving the body at home."[111] Similarly, Margaret Johnson confessed that when travelling to the Sabbath, it was not the bodies of Witches that would go forth to such places but their spirits instead.[112] Many times, spirit flight to the Sabbath was discussed in terms of being a dream or dreamlike. For instance, in 1608 an accused Frenchwoman named la Grande Lucye confessed that at times she only dreamed of the Sabbath, while other times she had been physically present. Similarly, in the Basque region it was noted that children so frequently claimed to have journeyed to the Sabbath while asleep that their parents often tied them to their beds or tried to keep them awake through the night so as to keep them home.[113]

Implements of Flight

Regardless of which type of flight, physical or spiritual, was used to get to the Sabbath, many accused Witches confessed to having made their aerial journeys astride a wide range of objects. While there were certain accounts of Witches flying unsupported, it was much more common to hear about them doing so with the aid of some sort of implement. Of course, in popular folklore Witches have become most associated with the broomstick. One of the very first recorded mentions of a Witch flying on a broom comes from 1454 when a French man, Guillaume Edelin, admitted to using one as a means of carrying himself to meet with the Devil at the Sabbath.[114] Additionally, the earliest known pictorial depiction of a Witch riding a broomstick was an illustration found in the margins of Martin le Franc's previously mentioned *Le champion des dames* (1440). But while the broomstick has become quintessential to the image of

---

111. Ginzburg, *The Night Battles*, 17.

112. Harland and Wilkinson, *Lancashire Folk-Lore*, 199.

113. Wilby, *Invoking the Akelarre*, 15.

114. Margaret A. Murray, *The God of the Witches* (Oxford: Oxford University Press, 1970), 90–91.

Witches in modern lore, historically it was not as prevalent as some of the other items found in the confessions of those accused.

Perhaps the simplest of objects used for conveyance to the Sabbath were common poles, sticks, and rods. For example, Ann Foster of Andover, Massachusetts, confessed that she and Martha Carrier flew to a Witches' meeting upon a pole. Foster added that the pole had broken mid-flight and caused both women to tumble to the ground.[115] Jeanette Clerc, an accused Witch from Geneva, Switzerland, confessed in 1539 that she rode to the Sabbath on a stick which she had enchanted by saying, "White stick, black stick, carry me where you should; go, in the Devil's name, go!"[116] In addition to sticks and poles, certain plants were also said to be used by Witches as vehicles for flight. Isobel Gowdie confessed that she would be carried away on pieces of straw or beanstalks after intoning, "[HORSE] and hattok, horse and goe, horse and pellattis, ho! ho!"[117] Still, other Witches were said to have used common farming tools, such as the unnamed woman from Eichstätt who confessed that she rode to the Sabbath on a pitchfork after speaking the words "Woosh! Up the chimney, up the window hole! In the name of the Devil, out and onward!"[118]

Besides inanimate objects, Witches were also believed to fly on the backs of various animals. For example, an accused man from Germany named Niclas Fiedler confessed in 1591 that he had mounted a billy goat, upon which he then flew to the Sabbath.[119] In Mora, Sweden, several people confessed in 1668 that after invoking the Devil at a crossroads, they were provided with beasts that carried them "over Churches and high Walls."[120] The trial transcript of an Italian woman named Matteuc-

---

115. Essex Institute, *Historical Collections of the Essex Institute*, vol. 3 (Salem, MA: G. M. Whipple and A. A. Smith, 1861), 68.

116. Monter, *Witchcraft in France and Switzerland*, 57.

117. Pitcairn, *Ancient Criminal Trials in Scotland*, vol. 3, 604. Pitcairn's brackets.

118. "The Witch-Hunt at Eichstätt," in *The Witchcraft Sourcebook*, 223.

119. "The Confession of Niclas Fiedler at Trier, 1591," in *The Witchcraft Sourcebook*, ed. Brian P. Levack (London: Routledge, 2015), 200.

120. Horneck, "An Account of What Happened in the Kingdom of Sweden in the Years 1669, and 1670," in Glanvill, *Saducismus Triumphatus*, 216.

cia Francisci described how riding upon a goat, "she would go to the said Night-Doings, always over graves, like a shriek of lightning."[121] In addition to animals, unsuspecting humans were also considered to be viable options for Witches to ride. For instance, an accused Polish woman named Małgorzata Kupidarzyna confessed that she had ridden to the Sabbath on the back of "Marcin, the labourer."[122] Anne Armstrong of Northumberland, England, testified in 1673 that Ann Forster had used an enchanted bridle to transform her into a horse. Forster then rode Armstrong to the Sabbath, later returning the girl to her human form by removing the bridle.[123]

Flying Ointment

Sometimes, in order to achieve flight, it was necessary for Witches to make use of what has become popularly known as *flying ointment* (sometimes referred to as *unguentum sabbati*). Traditionally said to be given to Witches by the Devil, this ointment was either smeared on their instrument of flight or directly on their body. Once the ointment had been applied, Witches would be able to fly forth to their assemblies. Such stories about flying ointments were a common feature among Witch Trial confessions from all across Europe—they were seemingly absent from the narratives of those accused in the early American colonies. Elizabeth Style of Somerset, England, confessed in 1664 that she would apply an oil to her forehead and wrists before being carried off to the Sabbath.[124] Meanwhile, a Polish woman named Anna Chałupniczka admitted that in order to fly, she had to first cover her body with an ointment.[125] Matteuccia Francisci recounted how she and other Witches would smear

---

121. "A Trial for Witchcraft at Todi," trans. Augustine Thompson, in *Medieval Italy: Texts in Translation*, ed. Katherine L. Jansen, Joanna Drell, and Frances Andrews (Philadelphia: University of Pennsylvania Press, 2009), 211.

122. Wyporska, *Witchcraft in Early Modern Poland 1500–1800*, 39.

123. Christina Hole, *Witchcraft in England* (London: B. T. Batsford Ltd., 1947), 124.

124. Joseph Glanvill, *Saducismus Triumphatus: Or, Full and Plain Evidence Concerning Witches and Apparitions* (London: S. Lownds, 1681), 139.

125. Wyporska, *Witchcraft in Early Modern Poland 1500–1800*, 39.

their bodies with an ointment and chant, "Ointment, ointment, bring me to the Night-Doings at Benevento, over water, over wind, over all bad weather!"[126] The accused Witches of Spain were said to anoint themselves with toad venom while saying, "Lord, I anoint myself in Thy Name, from henceforth I am to be one with the Devil. I am to be a demon and I must have nothing to do with God."[127] However, while flying ointments were frequently mentioned in Witch Trial confessions, it was rare for an actual recipe for one to be given. Despite this, learned authorities took it upon themselves to record the ingredients that they believed composed the alleged magical salve.

One of the oldest recorded recipes for flying ointment was provided by the German physician Johannes Hartlieb in his book, *Das Puch aller varpoten Kunst, Ungelaubens und der Zaubrey* (Book on All Forbidden Arts, Superstition, and Sorcery), which was written in 1475. Hartlieb explained that the ointment was composed of seven herbs, which had to be collected on particular days of the week. These herbs included heliotrope (borage) collected on Sunday, *Lunaria annua* or *rediviva* (annual or perennial honesty) collected on Monday, *Verbena* (vervain) collected on Tuesday, *Mercurialis* (spurge) collected on Wednesday, *Anthyllis barba-jovis* (Jupiter's beard) collected on Thursday, and *Adiantum capillus-veneris* (maidenhair fern) on Friday. The seventh herb, which was to be collected on Saturday, went unnamed, as Hartlieb did not want his readers attempting to recreate the ointment for themselves.[128] Recall, though, that Saturday is said to be ruled by the planet Saturn, which is also believed to have dominion over plants such as the nightshades—many of which would be featured in later recorded recipes.

---

126. "A Trial for Witchcraft at Todi," in *Medieval Italy: Texts in Translation*, 210.

127. Alfonso de Salazar Frías, "An Account of the Persons at the Auto de Fe," in *The Salazar Documents*, ed. Gustav Henningsen (Leiden: Brill, 2004), 116.

128. Joseph Hansen, *Quellen und Untersuchungen zur Geschichte des Hexenwahns und der Hexenverfolgung im Mittelalter* (Bonn: Carl Georgi, 1901), in P. G. Maxwell-Stuart, *Witch Beliefs and Witch Trials in the Middle Ages* (London: Continuum, 2011), 77–78.

While Hartlieb's flying ointment appears rather tame, a new precedent would be set in 1486 after the publication of the *Malleus Maleficarum*. Written by a German Catholic clergyman named Heinrich Kramer, the *Malleus Maleficarum* eschewed mentions of herbs in its description of flying ointment. Instead, Kramer focused explicitly on macabre ingredients such as the limbs of unbaptized children.[129] Recipes that emerged in the following years would combine similarly gruesome constituents with plants and herbs—most of which were poisonous. Thus, Girolamo Cardano provided a recipe in his 1550 book, *De subtilitate rerum*, which contained parsley, aconite, cinquefoil, and nightshade as well as the fat of young children and soot. Giambattista della Porta included two recipes in his book *Natural Magick* (1558), the first of which was nearly identical to Cardano's, while the second was composed of "sium, acarum vulgare, pentaphyllon, yellow watercress, common acorus, cinquefoil, the blood of a flitter-mouse, solanum somniferum and oleum, sleeping nightshade and oil."[130] Johann Weyer described an ointment in his 1563 book *De praestigiis daemonum et incantationibus ac venificiis* made from henbane, hemlock, darnel, deadly nightshade, and opium as well as funerary objects such as shreds of clothing belonging to the dead.[131]

The Sabbath in Art: Goethe's *Faust*

An artistic description of the Sabbath that is rich in detail regarding its location and timing, as well as the varied modes of transportation taken by Witches to get there, can be found in Johann Wolfgang von Goethe's tragic two-part play entitled *Faust*. The earliest form of the play, known as *Urfaust*, was developed between the years 1772 and 1775. However, it wasn't until 1808 that part 1 of *Faust* was first published. Part 2 was published posthumously after Goethe's passing in 1832. The play is based upon a German legend about a magician who, in his quest to gain knowl-

---

129. Heinrich Kramer and Jacob Sprenger, *The Malleus Maleficarum*, trans. Montague Summers (Mineola, NY: Dover Publications, 1971), 107.

130. Giambattista della Porta, *Natural Magick* (Germany: Black Letter Press, 2020), 611.

131. Hatsis, *The Witches' Ointment*, 189–90.

edge and power, sold his soul to the Devil. This legend, in turn, is said to have been inspired by the real life of a man named Georg, or John, Faust who was a disreputable professor and known magician. The very first surviving mention of Georg Faust can be found in a letter written by the Benedictine abbot and magician Johannes Trithemius and dated 1507. John Faust was known to Martin Luther, who referred to the man as one of the Devil's allies. In fact, Faust himself was said to call the Devil his brother-in-law.

In Goethe's version of the legend, the protagonist signs a pact with the demon Mephistopheles, who has promised to do everything asked of him if Faust will eventually serve him in hell. At a later point in the play, Mephistopheles takes Faust on an adventure to the Harz Mountains, where Witches and Wizards are eagerly gathering for their Walpurgis-nacht celebration. Mephistopheles offers Faust a broomstick to ride up the mountainside, but the man insists on walking. Along the way, they meet up with a will-o'-the-wisp, who Mephistopheles commands to guide their way. At the summit of the mountain, Faust observes brilliantly lit fires and crowds of people making merry. The Witches and Wizards sing:

> *The witches ride up to the Brocken Horn,*
> *The stubble is yellow, green is the corn!*
> *The rabble is gathered awaiting the call,*
> *Aloft sits Lord Urian ruling them all.*
> *Here is the path, over stick, over stone;*
> *The he-goat stinks, and it———s the crone.*[132]

While many of the Witches fly about, one character—who is noted to be only a half-Witch—laments that she is unable to fly like the others. She begs the other Witches not to leave her behind and explains that she has tried to reach the mountain's summit for the last three hundred years. In response, they tease her by singing:

---

132. Johann Wolfgang von Goethe, *Faust*, trans. Alice Raphael (Norwalk, CT: The Heritage Press, 1959), 154. Author's line.

A broomstick will carry you—so will a stick,
A pitchfork will carry you—a goat does the trick.
He who cannot raise himself to-day,
Lost forevermore must stay![133]

While Goethe's version of the Faustian legend was penned several centuries after the development of the Sabbath narrative, it speaks to its lasting presence in the public mind. Additionally, the version of the Sabbath presented is noticeably devoid of overt ecclesiastical ideals. Instead, Goethe focuses rather humorously on the more folkloric details, such as the implements used by Witches for flight. It's interesting to note that it was Goethe's play that introduced the Walpurgisnacht scene to the Faustian legend. In doing so, he helped popularize the association between the Brocken and the Witches' Sabbath. In fact, prior to *Faust*, the only published reference to Witches gathering atop the Brocken was in Johannes Präetorius's book *Blockes-Berges Verrichtung* (1668). In addition to referencing common beliefs regarding the Sabbath, Präetorius's book describes how these meetings take place on the Brocken and includes a vivid illustration depicting the mountaintop revelries. And it was this book that helped inspire Goethe in writing *Faust*, which would become the most celebrated interpretation of the German legend.

---

133. Goethe, *Faust*, 155.

Chapter 4
OVER THE HEDGE
AND THROUGH THE AIR

Folklore tells us that the Witches' Sabbath was held in a myriad of locations, that it occurred during the late hours of certain nights, and that Witches either traveled to these meetings in person or in spirit. But how do we go about applying this lore to our modern practices? Timing aside (we'll come back to this in chapter 8), the two most important questions are where does the Sabbath occur today and how do we get there? Well, first and foremost, as mentioned earlier in this book, within the practice of Traditional Witchcraft the Sabbath is experienced as an Otherworldly event that practitioners attend in spirit form. While there are ways that the Sabbath can be physically enacted in the material world, it is primarily interpreted as taking place within the hidden landscape of the Otherworld. Therefore, drawing inspiration from accounts of Witches' flying to the Sabbath, modern practitioners turn to the art of spirit flight. By leaving our physical bodies and traveling into the Otherworld, we gain access to the legendary assembly of Witches and spirits. But before a journey to the Sabbath is possible, it's important to have an understanding of the Otherworld itself—including the Sabbath's specific location within it. Of course, it is also inherently necessary to learn how to go about leaving your physical body and crossing into the realm of spirits. Without such knowledge, ventures into the Otherworld and attempts to find the Witches' Sabbath will prove to be futile at best and perilous at worst.

The Witches' Otherworld

What exactly is the Otherworld? That's a question that I'm not sure can be answered in one, concrete way. However, at its core, the Otherworld is a realm, or collection of realms, that exist separate (yet sometimes overlapped with) our own physical world. It is the place where many different types of spirits reside and where magical energy flows more freely. It is also the place where you will find the Witches' Sabbath. For practitioners of Traditional Witchcraft, the Otherworld is an important place and is often experienced as a home away from the mundane. In fact, it is often said that Witches stand with one foot in each of the worlds, straddling the mystical boundary that divides them. But where exactly is the Otherworld located, and what does it look like? Those are also both questions to which there are no easy answers or simple explanations. This is because the ways in which the Otherworld is experienced will always be entirely subjective to the individual and the culture within which they are operating. Consider for a moment how many different religions and spiritualities there are in the world, and how each one has their own variation of an Otherworld or afterlife. Witchcraft is no different in that, within its many different traditions, there are varying ideas regarding the specific nature of the Otherworld. Additionally, the Otherworld is highly fluid and its landscape shifts as easily as smoke in the wind. Thus, even on an individual level, a Witch might experience the Otherworld one way only to find it looks completely different upon returning another time.

The Three Worlds and the Hidden Landscape

Despite the Otherworld's mercurial appearance, it can be roughly divided into three different worlds: the Upperworld, Midworld, and Underworld. In the simplest of terms, the Upperworld is a heavenly realm where the gods reside, while the Underworld is the subterranean home of the dead. In between these two worlds exists the Midworld, which consists of both the physical plane of humans as well as a hidden Otherworldly landscape wherein the spirits of nature are housed. This trisected view of cosmology can be found to varying degrees throughout many different cultures.

For example, ancient Mesopotamians believed that their earthly world was sandwiched between a heavenly dimension of gods and an underground one that was populated by the spirits of the dead. Similarly, the Egyptians conceptualized their Otherworld as consisting of an Upperworld and Underworld. The latter, which was known as *Duat*, was the initial destination for the recently deceased. Here, spirits were tested to determine whether or not they were deserving of an afterlife. Those who were deemed worthy passed into the Upperworld, which was known as *Aaru*. And perhaps the most well-known and well-defined example of the three worlds model comes from Norse mythology, wherein there were believed to be nine different realms of existence, which in turn could be divided into an Upperworld, Midworld, and Underworld.

While the Upperworld and Underworld are both deserving of attention, for the purposes of this book we will be focusing exclusively on the Midworld, as this is where the Witches' Sabbath takes place. Sitting between the Upperworld and Underworld, the Midworld is the physical realm of humans and nature. However, there is another side to the Midworld beyond the mundane one, a hidden Otherworldly landscape that plays host to various spirits such as the *genius loci* (overall spirit of a given place), the *land wights* (individual nature spirits), and the Fair Folk. Additionally, it is within the folds of this hidden landscape, which exists parallel to or just behind our own, that the Witches' Sabbath can be found. Appearing quite similar to our own natural landscape, this Otherworldly version consists of forests, fields, mountains, and seashores. Therein one might find certain constructed features as well, such as churches, graveyards, crossroads, and stone circles. Consistent with the folklore, these spirit locales can all be potential candidates for the Sabbath ground.

The Axis Mundi

The three worlds are structured and centered along what is known as the *axis mundi*, or cosmic axis. Sometimes also referred to as the world tree, the axis mundi is a vertical line or roadway that runs through the Otherworld. Similar to the three worlds, there are variations of the axis mundi throughout different cultures. There are many examples of the axis mundi existing as a tree, such as the Norse *Yggdrasil*, the Mayan *Yaxche*, and the Sumerian *Huluppu*. Other times, though, the axis mundi appears in other forms. For example, Mount Olympus of Greek mythology can be viewed as a cosmic axis—with the gods residing atop the mountain (Upperworld), humans living around its base (Midworld), and the spirits of the dead resting underneath (Underworld).

When venturing into the Otherworld, the axis mundi not only acts as your cosmic map but as your spiritual roadway as well. You may ascend the axis mundi into the Upperworld, an act that is often envisioned as climbing the branches of a tree, hiking up a mountainside, or walking up a flight of stairs. Similarly, you might descend the axis mundi into the Underworld, which is typically visualized as crawling down the roots of a tree, lowering yourself into the depths of a cavern, or stepping down a flight of stairs. In the Midworld, you have the option of wandering in the cardinal directions of north, south, east, west, and all those in between. This can be experienced several ways, including hiking along paths or trails as well as trekking ancient tracks and roadways. Regardless of which path you take, each one leads back to the axis mundi at the center. Thus, the world tree becomes a sort of a home base for your Otherworldly journeys, including those to the Witches' Sabbath, where each one begins and ends.

EXERCISE
Axis Mundi Visualization

Having a thorough conceptualization of the axis mundi will be important moving forward. For this exercise, consider what you imagine the axis mundi to look like. Is it a tree or a mountain? Or is there some other imagery that speaks to you? Is there a variation of the axis mundi from your ancestral culture? Once you have an idea of what the axis mundi looks like for you, gather some drawing supplies and sketch it out. Alternatively, you could use paint or other artistic media to create your image. Don't worry if your artistic abilities are lacking; this is not about perfection but rather expression.

As you create your visual representation of the axis mundi, consider your other senses as well. If you were standing before the axis mundi, what would you hear? What would you feel? What would you smell? What would you taste? You may not have an answer for each of the senses and that's okay! Do your best. The more details you are able to put into your conceptualization of the axis mundi, the more vividly you'll be able to experience it later on when you're in the Otherworld.

The Witches' Compass Round

Within the modern practice of Traditional Witchcraft, the mapping of the Otherworld is often made manifest through a ritual known as *laying the compass round*. It is through this ritual that the practitioner intentionally taps into the axis mundi and creates a six-way crossroads. More specifically, the practitioner calls upon the spirits of each direction—north, south, east, west, above, and below—to open the roadways into each of their respective realms. Thus, the Upperworld, Underworld, and the hidden landscape of the Midworld become accessible. Once the compass has been laid, there are two main ways in which it might be engaged. First, the practitioner may stay in its center and make use of the currents of power flowing from each direction in order to work acts of magic. In this way, the spirits and virtues of the different worlds come together like the ingredients within a cauldron, coalescing to achieve a desired outcome. Second, the practitioner can travel in spirit along the roadways into the different worlds. While laying a compass round is not necessary for Otherworldly journeying, I find that it can be a powerful tool that has the potential to help ground the overall experience.

 EXERCISE
Laying the Compass Round

In today's practice of Traditional Witchcraft there are many potential ways for laying the compass round. The concept of the compass round comes from the late Traditional Witch Robert Cochrane (1931–66). Cochrane had his own specific way of laying a compass (see pages 62–63 of my book *The Crooked Path*), but this exercise will make use of my own personal method, which I find to be both simple and effective. You can follow the format I have provided, but the best results come from the elements being assigned to the directions in a way that makes sense to your local landscape. For example, where I live, we have a strong northern wind, so I assign air to that direction. But if you have a river to the north of your working space, it would make more sense to assign water to that direction. If you have difficulty with this, use your intuition and experiment with different options until you find the right fit.

Necessary Items
Incense of your choosing
White or black pillar candle
Palm-sized stone
Small bowl of water

To begin, locate each of the four directions (you can use the compass app on your phone for this). Then, starting in the north, stand with your feet firmly planted on the ground. In your hand, hold the burning incense, fan your fingers through the smoke and smell its rich scent. Close your eyes and take in a deep breath. Feel yourself reaching out to the spirits of the northern road. When you feel connected, say aloud,

I call to the spirits of the north, primal powers of air and wind. I kindly ask that you open the roadways into your realm. Come, join my compass round!

Move to the east, standing with your feet firmly planted on the ground. In your hand, hold the flickering candle, pass a finger quickly near the flame, and feel its heat. Close your eyes and take in a deep breath. Feel yourself reaching out to the spirits of the eastern road. When you feel connected, say aloud,

I call to the spirits of the east, primal powers of fire and flame. I kindly ask that you open the roadways into your realm. Come, join my compass round!

Move to the south, standing with your feet firmly planted on the ground. In your hand, hold the stone, run your fingers over its surface, and feel its solid mass. Close your eyes and take in a deep breath. Feel yourself reaching out to the spirits of the southern road. When you feel connected, say aloud,

> I call to the spirits of the south, primal powers of earth and stone. I kindly ask that you open the roadways into your realm. Come, join my compass round!

Move to the west, standing with your feet firmly planted on the ground. In your hand, hold the bowl of water, dip your finger in, and feel the coolness. Close your eyes and take in a deep breath. Feel yourself reaching out to the spirits of the western road. When you feel connected, say aloud,

> I call to the spirits of the west, primal powers of water and sea. I kindly ask that you open the roadways into your realm. Come, join my compass round!

Move to the center of the circle, standing with your feet firmly planted on the ground. Raise your arms above your head, spreading your fingers and reaching as high as you can. Close your eyes and take in a deep breath. Feel yourself reaching out to the spirits of the upper road. When you feel connected, say aloud,

> I call to the spirits above, primal powers of the Upperworld. I kindly ask that you open the roadways into your realm. Come, join my compass round!

Remain in the center of the circle with your feet firmly planted on the ground. Lower your arms toward the ground, spreading your fingers and reaching as low as you can. Close your eyes and take in a deep breath. Feel yourself reaching out to the spirits of the lower road. When you feel connected, say aloud,

> I call to the spirits below, primal powers of the Underworld. I kindly ask that you open the roadways into your realm. Come, join my compass round!

Continue standing in the center of the circle. Take in a deep breath and feel the magical currents flowing from each of the directions. Sense the ways in which these energies extend backward, along their respective roadways, disappearing in the depths of their realms. Sense the ways in which those energies coalesce in the center, forming the Otherworldly crossroads of the Witches. In the final chapter of this book I will discuss how to specifically utilize the compass round as a navigational tool for Otherworldly travel. For now, you can practice laying a compass round and working acts of magic in its center.

When you wish to end your ritual, it's polite to give thanks to the spirits of each direction and to bid them farewell. Start in the center, with your arms lowered toward the ground, and say aloud,

> *I give thanks to spirits below, primal powers of the Underworld. Until we meet again, I bid thee farewell!*

Remaining in the center of the circle, lift your arms above your head, and say aloud,

> *I give thanks to spirits above, primal powers of the Upperworld. Until we meet again, I bid thee farewell!*

Move to the west, extend your arms outward, and say aloud,

> *I give thanks to the spirits of the west, primal powers of water and sea. Until we meet again, I bid thee farewell!*

Move to the south, extend your arms outward, and say aloud,

> *I give thanks to the spirits of the south, primal powers of earth and stone. Until we meet again, I bid thee farewell!*

Move to the east, extend your arms outward, and say aloud,

> *I give thanks to the spirits of the east, primal powers of fire and flame. Until we meet again, I bid thee farewell!*

Finally, move to the north, extend your arms outward, and say aloud,

I give thanks to the spirits of the north, primal powers of air and wind. Until we meet again, I bid thee farewell!

Spirit Flight

In order to access the Otherworld, and subsequently the Sabbath itself, practitioners of Traditional Witchcraft employ the art of spirit flight, also sometimes called *transvection* or *hedge-crossing*. As noted earlier, the process of spirit flight involves the spiritual body of the Witch lifting from the physical one, allowing one's ethereal form to cross the boundary into the Otherworld. Spirit flight has often been compared to astral projection, and I believe the two are comparable, but that will of course depend on how you personally define each one. Regardless of what you might call it, folklore speaks of Witches with the power to fly. And just as Traditional Witches have woven various strands of other folkloric beliefs into their practices, so too has flight been honed and utilized. Of course, understanding the laws of gravity and keeping with the Otherworldly interpretation of the Sabbath, flying is accepted as occurring on a purely spectral level.

Learning the skill of spirit flight is a process, and it will take both dedicated practice and a great deal of patience. But before getting started, it's important to do away with some of the common preconceived notions regarding spirit flight. First, it is often mistakenly thought that spirit flight involves the complete disconnection between spirit and body. However, this is just not the case, as such a severance between the two only occurs at the time of one's physical death. Instead, your spirit will remain tethered to your body during Otherworldly journeys. As such, it is natural to retain some awareness of both your physical body and the general surroundings you left behind while your spirit is out and about. Second, it is frequently assumed that sensory input while in spirit form will be on par with that experienced while in the physical body. In reality, our five senses work differently on a spiritual level. Therefore, the way you see, hear, feel, smell, and taste things while engaged in spirit flight will be much different. None of this is to say that spirit flight or the resulting experiences of the Otherworld will not be vivid or distinct, but rather it is meant to combat unrealistic expectations that can lead to feelings of both pressure and disappointment.

With that in mind, the first step to achieving spirit flight is to become adept at creating and maintaining a trance state. By entering a trance, you shift your consciousness to a place that is somewhere between wakefulness and sleep. In such a place you are not fully aware of your physical body and surroundings, but you retain control of your mental, emotional, and spiritual faculties. As a result, the spirit becomes loose within the body, at which point it can be lifted up and sent forth. Thus, trance states, with their liminal powers, are utilized as the entry points into the process of spirit flight. And as Andrew Chumbley pointed out, it is at this intersection of waking, sleeping, and dreaming that we not only arrive in the Otherworld but at the Witches' Sabbath itself.

Brain Wave Frequencies and Trance States

It is impossible to discuss trance states without also discussing brain wave frequencies, as the two are largely one and the same. Every single thought, emotion, and behavior that we have is rooted in the communication between neurons inside of our brains. In order to communicate with one another, neurons fire electrical impulses that release neurotransmitters. When masses of these electrical pulsations become synchronized, they produce what are known as *brain waves*. Among many things, brain waves are responsible for our various states of consciousness. There are five types of brain waves, each corresponding to a different level of consciousness. Having a basic understanding of these brain waves is fundamental for learning how to go about inducing the trance state necessary for spirit flight.

Gamma (32–100 Hz): Gamma brain waves are experienced when we are engaged in learning, cognitive processing, or tasks that involve problem-solving.

Beta (13–32 Hz): Beta brain waves are experienced when we are wide awake, such as when we are going about our daily lives and using logical reasoning or linear thought.

Alpha (8–13 Hz): Alpha brain waves are experienced when our mind begins to relax, such as when we are resting or daydreaming.

Theta (4–8 Hz): Theta brain waves are experienced when we are significantly relaxed, such as when we are in a deep meditation or dreaming while asleep.

Delta (0.5–4 Hz): Delta brain waves are the slowest of the brain waves and are experienced when we are in a profound, dreamless state of sleep.

For the purposes of spirit flight, you'll need to shift your brain wave activity to a theta state. It's in theta that you'll find that liminal space between wakefulness and dreaming through which access to the Otherworld can be gained. While it might seem like you'd want to achieve the lowest brain wave activity for spirit flight, delta usually only occurs during deep, dreamless sleep. Therefore, you'll want to avoid going too deep into a trance state, in which case you'll most likely fall asleep. It should be noted that spirit flight can be achieved while in an alpha state, in which case your journey will be lighter, and thus you will have more control. However, you may be more prone to physical distractions in this state. In any case, there are many helpful techniques for shifting your brain waves and subsequently drifting into the trance state necessary for spirit flight, whether alpha or theta.

Deep Breathing

One of the most important tools for inducing a trance, and thus for spirit flight as well, is your own breath. Often overlooked because of its automatic nature, breathing possesses the power to dramatically affect our physical, mental, emotional, and spiritual states. When we mindfully focus on our breathing, taking nice, deep inhales and long, steady exhales, we stimulate our parasympathetic nervous system, which decreases both our blood pressure and heart rate, effectively promoting a sense of calm.

A full-bodied sense of calm is key to reaching the trance state associated with lowered brain wave frequencies. Luckily, it's relatively easy to learn and practice effective deep-breathing techniques. If you are already experienced with inducing a trance state, consider using the following exercises as a helpful review.

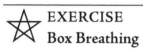

EXERCISE
Box Breathing

This exercise gets its name from the imaginary box or square whose four sides create the pattern of the breathing cycle you will be utilizing. To begin, take in a nice, deep inhale through your nose. As you take in this breath, feel your stomach push outward. Make sure not to force the breath, but rather allow your body to find its natural rhythm. Hold this breath for a second or two—don't hold it for longer than what is comfortable—and then let out a long, steady exhale through your nose or through your mouth. As you exhale, feel your stomach flatten back down. Hold again for a second or two before starting the cycle over. For the sake of practice, complete four to five sets of these breathing cycles. Once finished, take note of how you feel physically, mentally, emotionally, and spiritually.

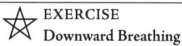

EXERCISE
Downward Breathing

The following breathing technique, which I refer to as downward breathing, is one that I first learned about in Christopher Penczak's book *The Inner Temple of Witchcraft*. To begin, you will want to sit or lie down somewhere comfortable and without distractions. Next, start the box breathing technique by taking in a nice inhale, holding for a moment, exhaling, and holding again. Repeat this cycle eleven more times, for a total of twelve repetitions, counting down in your mind as you go. By the time you reach the end, you will have hopefully achieved both mental and physical relaxation and entered into an alpha state. Now, take yourself even deeper into a trance state by repeating the process but with thirteen cycles this time, again counting down as you go along. When you reach the end of the second countdown, if successful, you will have entered into a theta state.

When you wish to come up from your trance state, perform the process backward. However, this time, instead of breathing, focus on becoming more cognizant of your body. Count up from 1 to 13, and then from 1 to 12. Allow yourself to come fully back into awareness. Wiggle your fingers and your toes, then your arms and legs. At whatever point you feel ready, slowly open your eyes and feel yourself return to the waking consciousness of a beta state.[134]

Progressive Muscle Relaxation

One of the goals in preparing for spirit flight is to become as minimally aware of your physical body as possible. While deep breathing allows your mind to still and move into a trance state, you may still find yourself distracted by your physical body. Whether you are experiencing tension in your muscles or you simply have a hard time sitting still, finding ways of relaxing your body is important to the process. Any bodily distractions will unwittingly keep you from fully engaging in spirit flight. In order to remedy this, I recommend using a technique known as *progressive muscle relaxation*. Essentially, this technique involves mindfully tensing various groups of muscles before releasing and experiencing a resulting sense of relaxation.

 EXERCISE
Progressive Muscle Relaxation

Begin by sitting or lying down in a comfortable position, making sure there are minimal distractions. Take in a nice inhale, hold, and then exhale. Continue to breathe steadily throughout this exercise—remember not to force your breathing but to let it come naturally. For each muscle group, tense for approximately eight to ten seconds before releasing. You do not need to tense your muscles too tightly, as doing so will cause strain and defeat the purpose of this exercise. Allow each muscle to tell you what it needs.

---

134. Christopher Penczak, *The Inner Temple of Witchcraft* (St. Paul, MN: Llewellyn Publications, 2002), 99–100.

1. Tighten the muscles in your feet by curling your toes down. Hold, taking in a nice breath. Exhale and release. Tell yourself, "My toes are now relaxed."

2. Tighten your calves by curling your toes upward. Hold, taking in a nice breath. Exhale and release. Tell yourself, "My calves are now relaxed."

3. Tighten your thighs by squeezing them together. Hold, taking in a nice breath. Exhale and release. Tell yourself, "My thighs are now relaxed."

4. Tighten your lower back by arching it upward. Hold, taking in a nice breath. Exhale and release. Tell yourself, "My lower back is now relaxed."

5. Tighten your stomach by flexing your abdominals. Hold, taking in a nice breath. Exhale and release. Tell yourself, "My stomach is now relaxed."

6. Tighten your shoulders by lifting them up to your ears. Hold, taking in a nice breath. Exhale and release. Tell yourself, "My shoulders are now relaxed."

7. Tighten your upper arms by pulling your triceps up toward your shoulders. Hold, taking in a nice breath. Exhale and release. Tell yourself, "My upper arms are now relaxed."

8. Tighten your lower arms by extending them out and locking your elbows. Hold, taking in a nice breath. Exhale and release. Tell yourself, "My lower arms are now relaxed."

9. Tighten your fingers by making a fist and squeezing gently. Hold, taking in a nice breath. Exhale and release. Tell yourself, "My fingers are now relaxed."

10. Tighten your jaw by opening your mouth as wide as you can. Hold, taking in a nice breath. Exhale and release. Tell yourself, "My jaw is now relaxed."

11. Tighten your eyes by shutting them tightly. Hold, taking in a nice breath. Exhale and release. Tell yourself, "My eyes are now relaxed."

12. Tighten your forehead by lifting your eyebrows as high as you can. Hold, taking in a nice breath. Exhale and release. Tell yourself, "My forehead is now relaxed."

13. Finish by taking another nice inhale. Hold. Then release, telling yourself, "My body is now fully relaxed."

Treading the Mill

While spirit flight is most commonly accessed through a state of profound relaxation brought on through stillness, there are other techniques that use movement to induce the trance state necessary to make Otherworldly journeys. Within the practice of Traditional Witchcraft, the primary method used in this regard is known as *treading the mill*. As with the earlier mentioned ritual of laying a compass round, treading the mill was created by Robert Cochrane. The ritual, while relatively modern, is reminiscent of the folkloric mentions about Witches performing circle dances at the Sabbath. As such, treading the mill involves repeated circumambulations around a central object, such as a bonfire, upon which one keeps their eyes focused. More specifically, one treads around the compass or circle, facing forward, with their shoulder parallel to the central object. The arm facing inward is extended out, with the index finger pointing at the central object. The head is tilted to the side and down so that it rests on the shoulder, and the line of sight is sent down the length of the arm and fixed upon the central object. Additionally, some practitioners use what's called the *lame step*—essentially dragging one foot behind them while they tread the mill. This particular movement is an homage to various spirits often worked with in Traditional Craft, such as Tubal Cain (an important figure in Cochrane's tradition), who are said to have a lame foot.

The purpose of treading the mill is twofold. First, it can be used as a way of summoning magical power. Through the movement and motions, the Witch draws energy from the Otherworld, from nature, and that which dwells inside themselves. These various currents of magical power then intermingle before being directed toward a specific goal, such as empowering a certain spell or ritual working. While not necessarily separate from the first, the second purpose for treading the mill is to induce a trance state. This is achieved through the monotonous motion of the circling paired with a fixed stare on the still object, creating a hypnotic effect. Additionally, the positioning of the head lightly limits the amount of oxygen flowing to the brain (not enough for this to be considered dangerous in any capacity), further producing an altered state of consciousness. It is the purpose for which the mill is tread that determines the direction, clockwise or counterclockwise, of the Witch's pacing. It is most common for the mill to be tread counterclockwise, as to go against the sun is symbolic of both the inverse nature of the Otherworld and the subversiveness of Witchcraft itself. That said, some practitioners find that treading the mill clockwise is useful when working beneficent forms of magic as well as attempting to bring about the increase of certain blessings. On the other hand, the sinistral pacing is best used for darker forms of magic such as hexing and banishing.

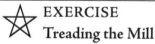 **EXERCISE**
Treading the Mill

For this exercise you will need an object to serve as a central focus. Within Traditional Witchcraft, it is common to use a stang (a forked ritual staff) for this purpose. Other times a bonfire, a small fire burning in a cauldron, or a simple candle will be used. Additionally, you could use a stone, a skull, or even a tree as a central focus.

To start, decide whether you are going to be pacing clockwise or counterclockwise. If you choose the former, stand with your right shoulder parallel to the central focus. Keeping your body facing forward, extending your right arm outward, pointing your index finger at the central focus. Turn your head to the side, cocking it back slightly so that your chin rests on your shoulder. Gaze down your arm and fix your sight on the central focus. Then, begin to slowly walk forward, making sure to maintain eye contact with the central focus. As you tread, you may wish to use the lame step. If that's the case, as you tread, allow your right foot (if pacing counterclockwise) or left foot (if pacing clockwise) to drag on the ground behind you.

Continue pacing, allowing the steady, monotonous motion to pull you into a deeper state of consciousness. Sense your mind becoming quiet and eyesight starting to soften. As you tread, be mindful of your breathing, keeping it smooth and rhythmic. After a while, you may notice that you start to gain speed in your circling. If this feels comfortable for you, continue to gather momentum. Otherwise, simply slow your movements.

Eventually, you will notice yourself entering into a deep trance. Using your intuition to sense when the gathered force is at its peak, stop dead in your tracks. Note that this will cause a dizzying, disorienting effect. If you are treading the mill to raise energy for a magical working, throw out your hands, feeling the power you have summoned projecting outward from your open palms. From here, the magic will go forth to where it is needed. If you are treading the mill to enter a trance or to cross the hedge, allow your body to collapse onto the floor. You can also gently lie down upon the ground if crumbling organically would cause injury or pain. Once you are lying down, use that gathered force to project yourself into a deep, meditative state. Later, in chapter 8, we will discuss how to use that force to fly forth out of your body in spirit form, over the hedge, and into the Otherworld.

Visualization

The ability to visualize, or to conjure up specific imagery within one's mind, is often considered a foundational skill necessary for the working of magic. While visualization is commonly associated with our ocular faculties, the ability to visualize actually includes all five of our senses—

sight, sound, touch, taste, and smell. In fact, for many people, the ability to see mental images in their mind can be quite difficult. Yet, at the same time, they might be able to hear, feel, smell, or even taste such images. And so, when talking about *images,* I'm not inherently referencing a visual image but rather the product of our *imagination,* which could be based in any of the five senses. Personal experiences with visualization vary, and some of your senses will naturally be stronger than others. So don't worry if you have a hard time picturing a particular object or scene within your mind. Instead, focus on which of your other senses might be creating that image in your mind. That being said, it is good to try practicing exercises that will strengthen your ability to visualize using each of your senses. Doing so will help you create more holistic images within your mind, which in turn will aid you not only in spirit flight but in your general practice of magic as well.

 EXERCISE
Hedgerow Visualization

In order to practice your visualization skills, whether you are new or looking to hone your already established abilities, this exercise is both simple and effective. As mentioned previously, the boundary between the physical world and the spiritual one is often described as a hedge. Because you will later be crossing this very hedge, it will prove useful to practice visualizing what this boundary looks like. To start this exercise, you may want to look on the internet for images of hedgerows in order to get a better feel for the different ways they might look. Then, close your eyes and take in a nice deep breath. Hold for a second or two, then let out a long, steady exhale. Allow your body and mind to become still. When you feel ready, focus your attention on the blank space above and between your two eyes (you can do this by gazing upward with your closed eyes). Next, call to mind the image of the hedgerow, projecting it onto that blank space above and between your eyes. Once the image of the hedgerow is in place, use your different senses to take notice of its finer details.

What does the hedgerow look like? Is it leafy or evergreen? How tall is it? Does the hedgerow make any sound? Does the wind whistle through its branches? Are there birds singing from nests hidden within? What does the hedgerow feel like? Are the leaves soft or glossy? Are there sharp thorns among the branches? What does the hedgerow smell like? Does the foliage have a particular scent? Is it woody or coniferous? Once your senses are fully engaged, try to hold the complete image of the hedgerow for two to three minutes.

 EXERCISE
Sabbath Ground Visualization

Once you have a handle on simple visualization, try your hand at something slightly more advanced. To begin, decide upon a location for the Sabbath ground, choosing from those mentioned in chapter 3. Once you have a location chosen, close your eyes and take in a nice deep breath. Hold for a second or two, then let out a long, steady exhale. Allow your body and mind to become still. When you feel ready, focus your attention on the blank space above and between your two eyes (you can do this by gazing upward with your closed eyes). Next, call to mind the image of the Sabbath ground, projecting it onto that blank space above and between your eyes. Once the image of the Sabbath ground is in place, use your different senses to take notice of its finer details.

First, are you indoors or outdoors? If you are indoors, are you in a house or a particular type of building, such as a church? If you are outdoors, are you in a forest? On a mountaintop or by the seashore? Look around you. What do you see? But don't just look—actually envision yourself walking about the Sabbath ground. As you do, notice what you feel. Is the air a certain temperature? Is there a magical charge to the atmosphere? Imagine that there is some type of fire present, whether it's a bonfire, fireplace, or a couple of candles. Reach out your hand and feel the warmth radiating from the flames. Imagine that the fire gives off an aroma of burning wood and herbs. What specific smells do you notice? Imagine that you can hear someone playing music nearby. What does the music sound like? Continue walking about the space and imagine that there is a table set with delicious foods and drinks. Select something from the table and taste it. What do you notice about its flavor? Once your senses are fully engaged, try to hold the complete image of the Sabbath ground for two to three minutes.

Music

Music is another tool that has the power to affect you on a physical, mental, emotional, and spiritual level. Consider the ways in which a sad song can cause your mood to dip or how a fast-tempo song can cause your body to move almost involuntarily. Just like deep breathing and other techniques can cause a shift in your brain waves, so can music. Listening to different sounds can allow you to enter trance states, both those that are frenzied and those that are still. The use of instruments such as drums, rattles, and flutes have long been used for spiritual purposes, specifically any work that involves the spirit journeying forth from the physical body and into the Otherworld.

If you wish to incorporate music into your practice of spirit flight, and your experiences of the Sabbath therein, there are a number of options to consider. First, what type of music will you be using? Songs with words can be useful at times and distracting at others, so it's important to get a feel for what works best for you. Additionally, consider the mood or theme of your journey, as different tempos can be used to encourage certain types of experiences. Second, will you be performing the music or will someone else? Playing your own instrument or singing your own songs can be a powerful way of entering a trance and traveling into the Otherworld, but this takes much practice and can be quite distracting for someone new to spirit flight. Therefore, it might be more helpful in the beginning either to have someone else provide the music for you or to play a recording. Third, if you are streaming music from your phone, computer, or other device, will you have a playlist or simply one song on repeat? It's also a good idea to make sure that your music will play uninterrupted by notifications and ads and that the device it's being played on is out of the way.

In addition to music featuring words and instruments, there is also a special type of music that is specifically meant for causing shifts in one's brain waves. Known as *binaural beats*, this music consists of a different tone played in each ear. These tones travel to the brain, where they meld into one singular beat that your brain then syncs to and creates an altered state of consciousness. You can find these binaural beats online by searching "binaural beat + (whichever state you'd like to achieve, in this case alpha or theta)." For the best results, you will need to wear a comfortable set of headphones.

Entheogens

Another set of tools that has been frequently used to help induce a trance state is *entheogens*—substances that have mind-altering properties and are used within a religious or spiritual context. There are many types of entheogens, ranging in both legality and safety, but they are most commonly derived from plants that possess psychoactive virtues. Please note that I do not endorse the use of illegal or dangerous substances. Entheogens, depending upon what they are, can be consumed (such as teas and tinctures), inhaled (such as smoke blends and incense), or applied topically (such as ointments). It's important to understand that the purpose of entheogens is not to "trip out," and abuse of such substances can have dire results both physically and spiritually. It's also important to understand that entheogens are not meant to be shortcuts into the Otherworld. Using these substances will not take the place of the hard work and dedication necessary to learn the ways of spirit flight. If you choose to make use of them in your practice, you must pair them with your own inherent abilities. While entheogens might cause a trance state on their own, without applying yourself to the process, you won't get very far, just as putting keys in the ignition might start a car, but without stepping on the gas and steering the wheel, you'll get nowhere.

Within the modern practice of Traditional Witchcraft, the most popular form of entheogen utilized is flying ointment. Pulled straight from the folklore of the Witches' Sabbath, these ointments contain various plant ingredients and are spread upon certain parts of the body in order to help lift the spirit from the body and send it off into the Otherworld. Many of today's flying ointments contain plant ingredients similar to the recipes of old, specifically the four members of the Solanaceae, or nightshade, family: mandrake (*Mandragora officinarum*), belladonna (*Atropa belladonna*), henbane (*Hyoscyamus niger*), and datura (*Datura stramonium*). It is vital to recognize and understand that each of the four nightshades contain deadly neurotoxins and therefore should never, under any circumstances, be taken internally—doing so can leave one anywhere from severely ill to dead in the ground. That being said, the four nightshades do hold psychoactive properties that can be absorbed through the skin with relative safety. Additionally, while the nightshades have a certain atavistic appeal, they are not the only entheogenic plants that can be used in the preparation of flying ointment. For example, two potent herbs commonly used in lieu of the nightshades are mugwort (*Artemisia vulgaris*) and wormwood (*Artemisia absinthium*).

If you find that you are drawn to the idea of working with flying ointment, it's imperative that you first do proper research, both in terms of ingredients and the effects they might have on your body. Make sure that you do not have any allergies to the ingredients and that there are no other potential health risks. Additionally, remember that all bodies are different; therefore, your use and results will naturally vary from someone else's. If you desire to work with an ointment containing any of the nightshade plants, I recommend that you purchase one prepared by a qualified herbalist rather than attempting to make one on your own. When looking for an ointment for sale, be sure to not only read through ingredient lists fully but also verify the creator's credentials as an herbalist. If you are really keen on the idea of creating your own flying ointment from scratch, you can use the non-toxic recipe provided below. In either case, whether purchasing a premade flying ointment or making your own, follow the provided instructions carefully. Wash your hands thoroughly before and after application, and only apply the ointment to safe areas, such as your temples and wrists (avoid mucous membranes).

If flying ointment doesn't quite appeal to you, there are other entheogenic options should you desire them. For example, certain herbs—such as mugwort and wormwood, along with many others—can be consumed as a tea or a tincture. In addition to plants that have psychoactive properties, those that have sedative qualities—such as skullcap, valerian, chamomile, and hops—are also quite useful for promoting a trance state. These herbs can be steeped in boiling water in order to make tea or soaked in vodka (or other high-proof alcohol) for an extended period of time to produce a tincture. I have had success with both teas and tinctures as entheogens, although I have found the latter to be slightly more potent. Additionally, a slightly less invasive and not often discussed type of entheogen is incense. The smoke of burning herbs, woods, resins, and oils can have profound effects on altering our consciousness, especially when the magical virtues of each ingredient align with the purposes of spirit flight. We can lightly breathe in some of this smoke, allowing it to take hold of our senses and to relax our bodies, and ride as spirits along its fragrant plumes. The following are a few of my tried and true entheogenic recipes, including an ointment, tea, tincture, and incense, all of which will aid in your Otherworldly travels to Witches' Sabbath.

Non-Toxic Flying Ointment Recipe
¼ cup wormwood

¼ cup mugwort

2 tablespoons vervain

2 tablespoons cinquefoil

2 tablespoons poplar leaf buds

Clean jar and lid

Grapeseed oil

Grated beeswax

Clary sage essential oil

Cheesecloth

To begin, you will need to create an oil infusion. Combine the wormwood, mugwort, vervain, cinquefoil, and poplar buds in a clean jar with a screw-on lid. Next, fill the jar with enough grapeseed oil to cover the herbs completely. Allow the herbs to steep in the oil for at least three lunar cycles, shaking the jar every so often. After the three lunar cycles have passed, strain out the herbs using a piece of cheesecloth. You will likely be using only a small portion of this oil infusion, so you can store the rest away for later use. Although, keep in mind that the oil will start to lose its potency after about a year.

The next step will be to combine the oil with a beeswax base. You'll want to follow a ratio of 1 part beeswax to 3 parts oil. Determine approximately how much ointment you'd like to make in order to find the appropriate amount of beeswax needed. Use a double-boiler system to melt the wax and then pour it into a clean container (such as a small metal tin or glass jar), filling it about ¼ of the way. Then stir in the oil, filling the rest of the container. Mix well and then blend in the clary sage essential oil, adding 10 to 15 drops for every 2 ounces of ointment. Like the oil infusion, the flying ointment will start to lose its potency after about a year's time.

When using the ointment, apply a small amount to the wrists, to the forehead, and behind the ears approximately 30 minutes before your journey. You'll know it's working when you start to feel zoned out and things around you seem to perceptibly slow down. When you've finished your journey, you can wash off any remaining ointment residue with soap and warm water.

> *Caution:* Be careful when applying herbal ointments to the body, as allergic reactions can occur! Always test a small amount on a patch of skin and discontinue use if a reaction does occur. Additionally, do not use this flying ointment if you are pregnant and/or breastfeeding, if you are allergic to ragweed, or if you have any type of heart condition.

Spirit Flight Tea Recipe

1 teaspoon black tea leaves

½ teaspoon mugwort

½ teaspoon chamomile flowers

½ teaspoon skullcap

Grind the ingredients together in a clean mortar and pestle, moving in a counterclockwise direction while focusing on your intention of leaving your physical body behind and traveling into the Otherworld. Place the loose mixture into a mesh tea ball and set it inside a sturdy mug. Boil water and then carefully pour it into the mug, covering the tea ball. Allow the tea to steep for 3 to 5 minutes before removing the tea ball. Make sure you give the tea time to cool before taking a sip.

Spirit Flight Tincture

Vodka

1 tablespoon wormwood

1 tablespoon damiana

1 tablespoon hops

Place each of the herbs into a clean jar with a screw-on lid. Pour enough vodka into the jar to cover the top of the herbs. Seal the jar tightly. Shake vigorously for a minute or two before placing the jar in a cool, dark place. Allow the herbs to steep in the vodka for three lunar cycles—shaking the jar every so often. After the three lunar cycles have passed, strain out the herbs and pour the tincture into a clean glass bottle (preferably one with a dropper). To use the tincture, place a dropperful under your tongue and allow it to absorb fully.

Hedge Witch Incense

1 tablespoon frankincense

1 teaspoon mugwort

1 teaspoon wormwood

1 teaspoon clary sage

1 teaspoon clove

1 teaspoon cinnamon

5 drops cedarwood essential oil

5 drops patchouli essential oil

Begin by using a mortar and pestle to grind the frankincense resin into a coarse powder. Then, add each additional herbal ingredient, one at a time, grinding them together as you go. Finally, add the essential oils to the powdered mixture, making sure to blend well. As the incense may still be wet from the oils, evenly spread out the mixture on a plate and allow it time to dry. Afterward, store the incense in a clean glass jar. When ready to use, this incense can be lit on fire and allowed to smolder, or it can be burnt upon an incense charcoal. In either case, make sure to burn the incense in a heat-proof container.

Chapter 5
A STRANGE AND
SINISTER COMPANY

At its very core, the Sabbath was a meeting of wayward souls, a dark gathering of Witches and spirits. It's easy to imagine the Sabbath as a place for the disenfranchised to congregate in order to bolster one another through the dark arts. Speaking to this sentiment, Matilda Joslyn Gage described the Witches' Sabbath as having been "the secret protest of men and women whom church and state in combination had utterly oppressed and degraded."[135] The Sabbath's company was largely composed of the Witches' themselves along with the Devil who stood as the grand master of it all. Beyond that, though, there were other visitors to the Sabbath, including children who may or may not have been Witches themselves. At times the Devil was joined by a Sabbath Queen who was variously seen as a specially selected coven member or as an Otherworldly being unto herself. There were also the occasional eldritch attendees, such as faeries and familiar spirits. In this chapter we will examine the appearances, dynamics, and specific roles of those who were said to haunt the Sabbath ground.

---

135. Gage, *Woman, Church and State*, 259.

The Coven

Hand-in-hand with the concept of the Witches' Sabbath is that of the coven. While the word *Sabbath* describes the meeting of Witches, a *coven* refers to the group of Witches itself. The term *coven* is a variant form of *covent*, which stems from the Latin *conventus*, meaning "assembly."[136] The variant form and its association with Witches arose in Scotland during the seventeenth century but did not gain popularity in the folkloric vernacular until two centuries later when it was included in Sir Walter Scott's 1830 book *Letters on Demonology and Witchcraft*. In his book, Scott wrote, "The witches of Auldearne, according to this penitent, were so numerous, that they were told off into squads, or *covine*."[137] The main purpose of these groups, just as the Sabbath itself, was to honor the Devil, work magic, and participate in sinful celebrations. It is possible that the coven also offered a sense of community, as evidenced by descriptions of playful Sabbath events; however, in most cases friendship did not appear to be the highest priority among the group's members. In fact, at times, dissension within covens seems to have been commonplace. Regardless of whether the dynamic was amicable or not, from the Middle Ages onward gathering in covens became the standard for Witches.

The size of individual covens varied greatly, ranging from small, intimate groups to those so large that members were often unknown to one another. However, it is difficult to determine exact numbers, as confessions rarely cited clear-cut figures, and it remains vague whether attendance at the Sabbath meetings necessarily reflected a singular coven's size. On the higher end of the spectrum, William Barker Sr. confessed in 1692 that he saw no less than 100 Witches present at the Sabbath meeting in Salem, all having been summoned by the resounding blast of

---

136. Online Etymology Dictionary, s.v. "coven (*n.*)," accessed February 5, 2021, https://www.etymonline.com/word/coven#etymonline_v_19191.

137. Walter Scott, *Letters on Demonology and Witchcraft* (London: George Routledge and Sons, 1884), 231.

a trumpet.[138] On the lower end, recall the meeting described by Gonin Depertyt at which there were only two other Witches present, besides himself and the Devil.[139] Later folklore holds that a coven's array is thirteen, a number which appears to have been somewhat common among trial confessions—especially those in Scotland. For instance Isobel Gowdie confessed that there were thirteen Witches in her coven from Auldearne.[140] Jonet Howat, who was also from Scotland, had confessed that "ther was thair presentt with the divell besyd hirselfe, quhhom he callit the prettie dauncer, the said Issobell Syrie, Mairie Rynd, Hellen Alexander, Issobell Dorward, and utheris whoise names shoe did not know, to the number of 13 of all."[141] Outside of these two cases, and in other regions, the number thirteen is often only hinted at, such as when Anne Armstrong reported having seen Anne Forster, Anne Dryden, and Luce Thompson present at the Sabbath along with ten other people she did not recognize.[142]

Within the coven, members sometimes filled certain roles or performed specific jobs at the Sabbath. In Scotland, the positions of maiden and officer of the coven were mentioned, although it remains a mystery what these positions entailed. Isobel Gowdie named Jean Mairten as the maiden of her coven and Johne Young as the officer.[143] Janet Breadheid, who was in the same coven as Gowdie, confessed in 1662 that before Young had taken up the role as officer, the position had belonged to her husband John Taylor.[144] Interestingly, the position of officer was not always reserved for men, as Bessie Weir of Paisley, Scotland, confessed in

---

138. "SWP No. 009: William Barker, Sr.," Salem Witch Trials Documentary Archive and Transcription Project, accessed February 5, 2021, http://salem.lib.virginia.edu /n9.html.

139. Monter, *Witchcraft in France and Switzerland*, 96.

140. Pitcairn, *Ancient Criminal Trials in Scotland*, vol. 3, 603.

141. Kinloch, *Reliquiae Antiquae Scoticae*, 114–15.

142. Hole, *Witchcraft in England*, 124.

143. Pitcairn, *Ancient Criminal Trials in Scotland*, vol. 3, 604.

144. Pitcairn, *Ancient Criminal Trials in Scotland*, vol. 3, 617.

1677 that she was the officer at several meetings.[145] Additionally, covens were at times described as having a ranking system that elevated certain members over others. When these ranking systems were in place, they were typically based on the age and prowess of the Witch. For example, accused Spanish Witches referred to the positions of *junior* and *senior* Witch, with the latter often having more status and privilege than the former.[146] However, ranking was also at times based on socioeconomic status. This was particularly true in France, where there were frequent mentions of tension between rich and poor Witches at the Sabbath. For instance, Ysabeau Richard confessed in 1615 that those Witches who were wealthy and of high social status were protected at the Sabbath, while those who were poor faced rejection from their affluent covenmates. She went on to say that the wealthy Witches were considered more important and enjoyed sitting at the table during the feast, while the poor Witches were kept at a distance.[147]

Although in some places the Sabbath had the feel of a more intimate and festive gathering where Witches were quite familiar with one another, in some instances it was quite the opposite. Out of fear of being recognized and potentially having their names escape the lips of persecuted covenmates, many Witches abided by a strict rule of anonymity. The most pronounced way in which this anonymity was demonstrated in accounts of the Sabbath was in the masks which some covens were said to wear. Nicolas Remy pointed out this custom when he wrote, "For they think they have no small cause to fear lest those who have been tried and found guilty of witchcraft should be induced by torture to betray their accomplices to the Judge; and for this reason they go masked to the Sabbat."[148] In 1612, a French woman named Claudon Bregeat further elaborated on the matter of disguises, confessing that most of the Witches in her coven

---

145. Glanvill, *Saducismus Triumphatus*, 291.

146. Frías, "An Account of the Persons at the Auto de Fe," in *The Salazar Documents*, 126.

147. Robin Briggs, *The Witches of Lorraine* (Oxford: Oxford University Press, 2007), 139.

148. Nicolas Remy, *Demonolatry*, trans. E. A. Ashwin (Mineola, NY: Dover Publications, 2008), 61.

wore masks made of linen, headdresses, or even hats pulled low over their faces in order to hide their true selves. Additionally, she mentioned a rather unique practice within her coven used to protect the identity of individual Witches. Bregeat explained that during the Sabbath dance, one coven member stood in the center and watched carefully for any Witch who dared try catching a glimpse of the others' faces. She noted that as a consequence, if a member of the coven was caught making such a faux pas, they would be pushed away violently.[149]

Children at the Sabbath

Among those who attended the Witches' Sabbath were a surprising number of children, ranging in age from infant to adolescent. Accounts of trials involving suspected child Witches can be found throughout Europe and in the early American colonies. However, in some areas, such as Sweden and Spain, the number of accused children was exceptionally high. In these areas, children regularly came forward with colorful stories about how they had traveled to nocturnal assemblies. Whether it was because of their wild imaginations or because they were being extorted by adults with ulterior motives, children seemed almost eager to share their experiences at the Sabbath. But in the minds of the persecutors and writers of the time, the vast number of child Witches was merely the result of the Devil seeking to corrupt those who were most impressionable. For instance, Pierre de Lancre noted that the Devil often sought out children because they were "most easily won over."[150]

For children, the journey to the Sabbath was typically instigated by their parents who brought them along or by unrelated Witches who kidnapped them from their beds. For example, the accused Witches in Mora, Sweden, gave the following account: "When the Children were asleep they [Witches] came into the chamber, laid hold of the Children, which straightaway did wake, and asked them whether they would go to a feast

---

149. Robin Briggs, *Witches & Neighbors* (New York: Penguin, 1996), 40.

150. De Lancre, *On the Inconstancy of Witches*, 309.

with them? To which some answered, Yes, others, No, yet they were all forced to go."[151] On the Spanish side of the Basque region, it was said that Witches would convince children to visit the akelarre by bribing them with fruit and asking if they would like to go someplace where they would have great fun with other children.[152] De Lancre added that Witches render children defenseless to being taken after laying hands on their faces or feeding them poisoned apples or bread made from black millet. As a result of this bewitchment, children would burn with a great desire to leave for the Sabbath.[153]

The extent to which children participated in the Sabbath activities is largely unclear, although it appears that they most commonly sat on the sidelines and simply watched the adult Witches engage in their debauchery. In Spain it was said that children could not become full-fledged Witches until they had reached the *age of discretion*—the age at which the Catholic Church believed a child was capable of making moral decisions and could therefore be judged for their sins. Thus, any child brought to the Sabbath was given a tiny switch and tasked with watching over the coven's toads and any other supplies used to make poison. It seems that these children were allowed to participate in dancing, though, as it was noted how they were carried piggy-back style by the older Witches during the frolicking.[154] In Sweden, child Witches were not allowed to sit at the table during the Sabbath feast. Instead, they had to eat their meal while standing near the entrance to the great house that sat in the center of Blåkulla.[155] Thankfully, children were also excluded from sexual encounters. De Lancre pointed out that demons wouldn't make explicit pacts

---

151. Horneck, "An Account of What Happened in the Kingdom of Sweden in the Years 1669, and 1670," in Glanvill, *Saducismus Triumphatus*, 317–18.

152. Frías, "An Account of the Persons at the Auto de Fe," in *The Salazar Documents*, 112.

153. De Lancre, *On the Inconstancy of Witches*, 97.

154. Frías, "An Account of the Persons at the Auto de Fe," in *The Salazar Documents*, 113–14.

155. Horneck, "An Account of What Happened in the Kingdom of Sweden in the Years 1669, and 1670," in Glanvill, *Saducismus Triumphatus*, 322.

with anyone who hadn't yet reached puberty (which the Church considered to be an appropriate age for marriage at the time).[156]

The stories provided by children regarding their visits to the Sabbath often had devastating effects on their families, becoming damning evidence against their own parents. For example, among the evidence against Margueritte le Charpentier, who was tried for Witchcraft in La Bourgonce, France, in 1620, were the stories that her son had told his school peers. According to the boy, whose name was Cesar, he and his mom had been carried up their chimney by a black dog who took them to a fine room where they feasted on a surplus of meat. Cesar added that he, his mom, and the dog all ate off the same plate and that they also danced and performed marvels. Unsurprisingly, Margueritte denied her son's claims and blamed the other children for him making up such lies. However, she eventually caved to interrogators when she learned that Cesar had made direct confessions which implicated her.[157] A century earlier, in 1597, the charges against Didier Pierrat of Saulcy-sur-Meurthe, France, were reinforced when his eight-year-old daughter reported how he had taken her to Sabbath. She explained how her father flew on a broomstick with her on his back to a mountaintop, where they ate meat and she watched him dance with a "black man."[158]

The Devil

The Devil served many roles at the Witches' Sabbath, the most important of which was that of grand master or overseer of the rites and festivities. It was in his honor that assemblies were held, and the events therein were enacted in his name. In a more active role, the Devil's primary function was as an initiator, awakening would-be Witches to their power. Additionally, he taught those at the Sabbath the ways of Witchcraft—specifically malefica—and how to use it in order to achieve their desires as well as his own. As the head of the Sabbath's company, the Devil appeared in

---

156. De Lancre, *On the Inconstancy of Witches*, 231.

157. Briggs, *The Witches of Lorraine*, 133–34.

158. Briggs, *Witches & Neighbors*, 234.

many different forms—including human and animal, as well as hybrid-
ized forms of both. He was described by the accused in various ways,
ranging from surprisingly regal or whimsical to horribly ugly and monstrous. From those accounts, it would seem that the Devil was an incredibly proficient shape-shifter, skilled in the art of metamorphosis. To that
end, de Lancre noted in his writing that the Devil "does not keep the same
appearance throughout; all his actions consist of changing his appearance,
since he never assumes a consistent identity; he is nothing but illusions,
deception, and fraud."[159]

When he would appear in human form, the Devil was typically
described as being a "black" or "dark" man. It is unclear whether those
descriptions were meant to denote his skin color or other physical features. Mary Toothaker, of Andover, Massachusetts, confessed in 1692
that the Devil had appeared to her as a "tawny man."[160] In this particular
case, Toothaker's vision of the Devil was directly related to the intense
fear of the surrounding Indigenous peoples (specifically the Wampanoag
tribe) at the time. It is certainly not out of the realm of possibility that
the designation of the Devil as a black or dark man could have had similar racist and xenophobic connotations. In other places, though, the Devil
was referred to as a "man in black," this time focusing on his clothing
rather than his physical characteristics. For example, Elizabeth Style confessed that she and three other Witches met with the Devil who looked
like a man dressed in black clothes.[161]

Conversely, the Devil was also said to wear brightly colored clothing
at times. The accused Witches of Mora, Sweden, claimed that the Devil
appeared to them as a man with a red beard wearing a gray coat, gartered
red and blue stockings, and a high crowned hat wrapped in linens of

---

159. De Lancre, *On the Inconstancy of Witches*, 96.

160. "SWP No. 128: Mary Toothaker," Salem Witch Trials Documentary Archive and
     Transcription Project, accessed February 5, 2021, http://salem.lib.virginia.edu/n128.
     html.

161. Glanvill, *Saducismus Triumphatus*, 143.

diverse colors.[162] Meanwhile, Gonin Depertyt of Switzerland mentioned in his confession that the Devil came to the Sabbath dressed in red.[163] Barbara Schluchter of Würzburg, Germany, confessed in 1617 that the Devil was a "beautiful young man with a black beard, red clothing, green stockings and black hat, with a red feather upon it."[164] Additionally, the Devil was often described as exuding a sense of royalty—wearing fancy clothing and sitting upon a throne. For instance, Walpurga Hausmännin of Dillingen, Germany, confessed in 1587 that the Devil appeared as a big man with a gray beard, richly attired and sitting in a chair like a great prince.[165] Hausmännin's description was echoed in the confessions of accused Spanish Witches who stated that the Devil sat on a great throne in royal dignity.[166]

When taking on bestial form at the Sabbath, the Devil seems to have had a preference for assuming the guise of a billy goat. Nicolas Remy explained that when the Devil wished to be worshiped by his disciples, he took on the form of a goat due to the fetid smell emitted by said creature.[167] However, the animal shape chosen by the Devil was also reflective of variances in regional fauna. For example, at one of the Sabbath meetings attended by Isobel Gowdie, the Devil appeared as a roebuck.[168] Meanwhile, a Polish man named Jan confessed in 1727 that the Devil had approached him in the guise of a wolf.[169] The Devil was also capable of taking on the form of an animal-human hybrid. For example, Agnes Sampson gave numerous descriptions of the Devil, among them being one in which he was said to have had a terrible face with a beak-like nose

---

162. Horneck, "An Account of What Happened in the Kingdom of Sweden in the Years 1669, and 1670," in Glanvill, *Saducismus Triumphatus,* 316.

163. Monter, *Witchcraft in France and Switzerland,* 96.

164. Lyndal Roper, *Witch Craze* (New Haven, CT: Yale University Press, 2004), 87.

165. "The Confessions of Walpurga Hausmännin, 1587," in *The Witchcraft Sourcebook,* ed. Brian P. Levack (London: Routledge, 2015), 194.

166. Frías, "An Account of the Persons at the Auto de Fe," in *The Salazar Documents,* 114.

167. Remy, *Demonolatry,* 72.

168. Pitcairn, *Ancient Criminal Trials in Scotland,* vol. 3, 603.

169. Wyporska, *Witchcraft in Early Modern Poland 1500–1800,* 62.

and burning eyes as well as hairy hands and legs that had claws like a grif-fin.[170] Additionally, Isabel Becquet reported that at her Sabbath the Devil had assumed the likeness of a dog standing on his hind legs, with two great horns and human hands.[171] Horns were a common feature ascribed to the Devil, and de Lancre noted that a general opinion among Witches was that the Devil had three horns, the middle of which was some sort of light that served as a source of illumination at the Sabbath.[172]

Queen of the Sabbath

In addition to the Devil, the Sabbath was also at times presided over by a woman. The title given to this woman occasionally varies. For example, Isobel Gowdie alluded to the special position of coven maiden. Addition-ally, when discussing the Sabbath in 1697, a young man named James Lindsay from Paisley, Scotland mentioned the presence of a woman named Antiochia. It was noted that this woman was the Devil's wife.[173] However, more often than not the female leader was referred to as the *Sabbath Queen*. Throughout trial confessions from Europe and the early American colonies, there are occasional references to a Witch who had obtained an elevated status within the coven and thus received special favors or attention from the Devil. Typically, this was a Witch who had demonstrated a proclivity for malefica greater than those of her coven-mates. The position of queen could be a permanent one, and such was the case in Salem when the Devil supposedly granted Martha Carrier the grand title of Queen of Hell.[174] Though, it seems that the position of Sab-bath Queen was usually only a temporary one, being passed on from one Witch to another over time. For instance, in eighteenth-century Poland

---

170. Pitcairn, *Ancient Criminal Trials in Scotland*, vol. 1, 240.

171. "The Confessions of Witches in Guernsey, 1617," in *The Witchcraft Sourcebook*, 213.

172. De Lancre, *On the Inconstancy of Witches*, 96.

173. *A Relation of the Diabolical Practices of Above Twenty Wizards and Witches of the Sher-iffdom of Renfrew in the Kingdom of Scotland* (London: Hugh Newman, 1697), 18.

174. "SWP No. 087: Mary Lacey, Jr.," Salem Witch Trials Documentary Archive and Tran-scription Project, accessed February 5, 2021, http://salem.lib.virginia.edu/n87.html.

a woman named Oderyna was said to have served as a Sabbath Queen, but the title was later inherited by someone else—a woman named Niewitecka—after her execution in 1737.[175]

In her appearance, the Sabbath Queen was normally characterized by her distinctive beauty and regal attire. Jeanette d'Abadie noted in her 1609 confession that the Devil always selected the prettiest women to be the Sabbath Queen.[176] In Spain the queen was said to wear an elaborate gold chain around her neck, with each link along its length depicting the Devil's face.[177] Meanwhile, in Poland she was described as wearing a gold crown and being surrounded by children.[178] In another Polish account, the queen's crown was replaced by a pair of golden horns.[179] Marion Grant of Aberdeen, Scotland, confessed in 1597 that she had attended dances at which the Devil was present with a woman dressed in a white waistcoat who was known as "Our Lady."[180] Margaret Talzeor of Alloa, Scotland, mentioned in 1658 that there had been a mysterious woman at the Sabbath who was dressed in a green waistcoat with gray tails.[181]

The role of the Sabbath Queen in some instances seems to have been a passive one, with the queen having little to do with coven leadership. For example, one of the primary honors given to those named as queen was a seat next to the Devil during the Sabbath feast. In this sense, while the Witch in question may have been chosen for her prowess in the malefic arts, her position as Sabbath Queen was less about power and more about pageantry. However, this was not always the case, as the queen was at times shown to play more important parts at the Sabbath, including

---

175. Wyporska, *Witchcraft in Early Modern Poland 1500–1800*, 39.

176. De Lancre, *On the Inconstancy of Witches*, 239.

177. Frías, "An Account of the Persons at the Auto de Fe," in *The Salazar Documents*, 122.

178. Wyporska, *Witchcraft in Early Modern Poland 1500–1800*, 39.

179. Wyporska, *Witchcraft in Early Modern Poland 1500–1800*, 184.

180. The Spalding Club, *Miscellany of the Spalding Club*, vol. 1 (Aberdeen, Scotland: Spalding Club, 1841), 171.

181. R. Menzies Fergusson, "The Witches of Alloa," *The Scottish Historical Review* 4, no. 13 (1906): 40–48.

taking on elevated roles during rituals. The accused Spanish Witches reported that during the Black Mass, the Queen of the Akelarre would sit by the Devil's side, where she collected offerings. In one of her hands she held an alms box and in the other she held a pax painted with an image of the Devil's face.[182] De Lancre notes that the grand mistress, or Sabbath Queen, aided in the initiation of children as Witches. Specifically, she instructed the children on what to do during the ritual and helped them to recite the proper words of renunciation.[183] In Scotland, Isobel Gowdie further hinted at the queen's prominence during rituals and magical workings when she expressed that "we doe no great mater without owr Maiden."[184]

Familiars

Yet another group of beings who could be found at the Witches' Sabbath were spirits known as *familiars*. These spirits served as assistants and advisors to Witches, having typically appeared shortly before or after the Witches had been initiated by the Devil. Familiars provided the Witch with a number of services, including to help carry out their evil biddings. Oftentimes these spirits appeared in the shape of an animal such as a cat, dog, bird, or toad, but they were also capable of taking on a human form. The exact nature of familiars fluctuates throughout folklore, as they were variously described as being demons, angels, faeries, or even spirits of the dead. Mentions of familiars at the Sabbath are admittedly less frequent in comparison to those regarding other Sabbath attendees. Despite this, the mentions that can be found are both fascinating and quite telling of the overall character of familiars. For example, while discussing the members of her coven, Isobel Gowdie mentioned that each one had a spirit who waited upon them. While she never explicitly states that these spirits were present at the gatherings she attended, Gowdie did provide a name

---

182. Frías, "An Account of the Persons at the Auto de Fe," in *The Salazar Documents*, 122.

183. De Lancre, *On the Inconstancy of Witches*, 400.

184. Pitcairn, *Ancient Criminal Trials in Scotland*, vol. 3, 610.

and description for each of the Witches' familiars.[185] The intimate details given suggest she had actually encountered the coven's familiars herself, which would have presumably occurred while at the Sabbath.

Allusions to familiars at the Sabbath were most common in the trial records of Great Britain, but they did occasionally show up in those of other countries as well. In Spain, for example, Witches were given toads as familiars, and those creatures were present at the Sabbath, where they were closely watched by the children in attendance. During the Sabbath, the toads were milked for poison, which was then used by the coven in various acts of malefica. The presence of familiars was also implicated in references to devils or demons at the Sabbath. For instance, in addition to the Witches and Lucifer, it was mentioned in the confession of Matteuccia Francisci that there were "hellish demons" among those gathered at the night-doings.[186] In the trial of Johannes Junius, it was described how he would meet with his *paramour*, a term used to describe a sort of attending spirit that usually carried romantic or sexual connotations. Junius had confessed that his paramour, who was named Vixen, was present at the Sabbath when he was initiated as a Witch. Additionally, Vixen promised that she would take him to other gatherings of Witches in the future. In a similar fashion, Vicencia la Rosa confessed that her familiar, named Martinillo, brought her to the Sabbath.[187] Furthermore, Walpurga Hausmännin confessed to having ridden to the Sabbath with her paramour upon a pitchfork. Taking these instances into account, it would appear that familiar spirits also functioned as a means of transportation, guiding Witches to their Sabbath meetings.

Faeries

In addition to the aforementioned attendees, faeries were sometimes included among the Sabbath's company. As we discussed earlier in this book, there has been considerable overlap between the folklore of Witches and that of the faeries. Included in this overlap are concepts regarding gath-

---

185. Pitcairn, *Ancient Criminal Trials in Scotland*, vol. 3, 606.

186. "A Trial for Witchcraft at Todi," in *Medieval Italy: Texts in Translation*, 211.

187. Henningsen, "'The Ladies from Outside,'" in *Early Modern European Witchcraft*, 198.

erings of faeries and those of Witches. There are many similar elements between the Witches' Sabbath and the Faerie Sabbath, including initiatory rituals, magical workings, feasting, music, dancing, and even sexual congress. Despite their commonalities, though, these two types of Sabbaths remain distinctly separate events. With that in mind, it's rare to find folkloric mentions of faeries attending the Witches' Sabbath. On the other hand, there are a number of references to Witches having visited the Faerie Sabbath. For instance, recall from chapter 1 the journeys to the faerie realm made by those such as Isobel Gowdie, Agnes Cairnes, and Alison Pearson, during which they witnessed and participated in acts similar to those at the Witches' Sabbath. Additionally, consider the case of Bessie Dunlop, an accused Witch from Ayrshire, Scotland. Dunlop confessed in 1576 that she had been approached by a group of twelve "gude wychtis [wights]" who "dwelt in the Court of Elfame." These wights, or faeries, asked Bessie to go with them—presumably to Elfame where she would have attended a Faerie Sabbath. However, Bessie turned down their offer, upon which they disappeared in a tempestuous blast of foul wind.[188]

At their Sabbath, faeries operated much like the Witches themselves, feasting, dancing, and making magic. Consider Alison Pearson's references to the merrymaking she witnessed among the faeries in the Court of Elfame. When it came to magic, references to the Faerie Sabbath contain instances of both malefic and beneficent workings. Isobel Gowdie noted that when she "wes in the efles houssis," she saw the faeries creating *elf arrows* or *elf darts*, which she and her coven members later used to cause bodily harm to their enemies.[189] On the flip side, an unnamed woman from Alcamo, Italy, confessed in 1627 that during her meeting with the faeries, they would go from house to house dancing and eating food while simultaneously providing blessings to the inhabitants. She noted that upon their departure, the faeries would say, "Stop the dance and let pros-

---

188. Pitcairn, *Ancient Criminal Trials in Scotland*, vol. 1, 52–53.
189. Pitcairn, *Ancient Criminal Trials in Scotland*, vol. 3, 607.

perity increase!"[190] Additionally, the Faerie Sabbath was presided over by a queen and king (although they did not always appear together), similar to the way in which the Devil and Sabbath Queen ruled the Witches' meetings. The queen and king were treated with reverence and looked upon as providers of both physical and spiritual fulfillment. Recall that those present at the meetings led by Madame Oriente received not only a plethora of food but knowledge of the magical arts as well. In 1598, Andro Man of Aberdeen, Scotland, reported that while meeting with the Queen of Elfame, she promised that not only would he come to "knaw all things, and suld help and cuir all sort of seikness," but that he would also be well entertained and provided with food.[191]

The Sabbath in Art: Francisco Goya's *El Aquelarre*

Since the concept emerged, there have been countless artistic representations of the Sabbath and its various attendees. By far one of the most well-known of these works is Francisco Goya's painting *El Aquelarre*. During the years 1797 and 1798, Goya created six oil paintings devoted to the theme of Witchcraft, including *El Aquelarre*. It is believed that these six paintings may have been commissioned by the Duke of Osuna, as he and his wife purchased the paintings shortly after they were completed. Goya's depictions of Witches were, in part, a critical commentary on superstitious belief, which still persisted among rural communities and the lower-class even after the Age of Enlightenment had begun.

El Aquelarre depicts a gathering of Witches seated around the Devil in a barren, hilly landscape.[192] Of course, this is the very meadow of the goat as described in Spanish Sabbath folklore. The Witches are variously aged, some appearing slightly younger than others, but each with a

---

190. Henningsen, "'The Ladies from Outside,'" in *Early Modern European Witchcraft*, 197–98.

191. The Spalding Club, *Miscellany of the Spalding Club*, vol. 1, 119.

192. A zoomable photo of *El Alquelarre* is hosted on Wikimedia Commons: https://commons.wikimedia.org/wiki/File:Francisco_de_Goya_y_Lucientes_-_Witches_Sabbath_-_Google_Art_Project.jpg.

withered, distorted face. Instead of being menacing in their countenance, these Witches appear rather silly and simple, perhaps representing the superstitious beliefs Goya was criticizing in this painting as well as in his other work. Together, the Witches sit in a circle, adoring the Devil, who is seated in the center. He wears the guise of a large black he-goat, sitting erect with big, luminous yellow eyes. His horns are crowned with a garland of verdant oak leaves, signifying his rule over the Sabbath meeting. The Witches appear quite causal in their positioning, with one of them half lying down. Unlike the stories of animosity among members, given the way these Witches are situated closely, it would seem that this coven is relatively harmonious, so to speak. Above the group, the sky is an inky blue-black across which bats flitter to and fro, perhaps spirits in their own right. Illuminated by the light of a waxing crescent moon, the Witches are in the process of dutifully offering up sacrifices to their Master. As per the darkest of folklore, these offerings are the bodies of dead or dying children. The stiff, decomposing body of a child lays on the ground nearby, while the legs of an infant stick out from under one of the Witches' clothing. Two of the Witches hold aloft the bodies of two more children—one significantly emaciated and skeletal, while the other is still fleshy and fresh. In the background, three nondescript small bodies hang from a post.

Despite Goya's attempts to portray Witches as ugly and foolish, there is something about *El Aquelarre* that is just the opposite—beautiful and serious. Goya's intent may have been to depict a group of deluded women who, in their desperation and folly, have turned themselves over to the Devil, even offering up children as a sacrifice to appease their master. Yet it's clear in the painting that these Witches believe in what they are doing: they have come together in the night to find their power, something that makes this representation of the Sabbath particularly alluring rather than repulsive. And so, while he may have been criticizing the continued presence of superstition among the general public, his work also provided visual fodder for those very same beliefs. And today, *El Aquelarre* continues to be one of most prominent artistic representations of the Witches' Sabbath.

Chapter 6
THE SABBATH CIRCLE

One of the key elements of Traditional Witchcraft is working with spirits in both the physical realm and the Otherworld. Spirits can be encountered in many different places, but one of the most centralized locations for such communion is at the Witches' Sabbath. At the Sabbath, today's practitioners can meet with various types of spirits in order to work magic, learn new skills, strengthen bonds, and join together in the ecstatic festivities classic to these nocturnal gatherings. In the previous chapter I discussed the assorted attendees of the Sabbath as they appear within folklore, including the coven of Witches, the Devil, and the Sabbath Queen as well as faeries and familiars. In modern practice, when visiting the Witches' Sabbath, you will naturally come across many of these same beings. However, the types of spirits present at the Sabbath will largely depend on the relationships you have with them. Thus, if you don't have a working relationship with the Devil in your Craft, he will be unlikely to show up at any meeting you attend. That being said, there may be times when unexpected guests arrive at the Witches' Sabbath, for better or worse. In any case, it's important for you to know about the spirits you might come across and how to safely work with them—or not work with them—while at the Sabbath.

Deities

In Sabbath lore, the gatherings of Witches were normally headed by a chief spirit, most commonly the Devil. Although, as discussed earlier, there were instances, such as Faerie Sabbaths, in which the leader was a female spirit. It is quite evident in the folklore that these particular spirits were and are of special importance. Beyond their elevated status as Sabbath leaders, these spirits had a certain persona that set them apart from the rest of the attendees. From a modern perspective, these spirits could be labeled as deities. Of course, this will hinge on how you personally define the term deity, but for the purposes of this book I will simply be defining deity as a spirit of an exalted position. Consistent with folklore, the Sabbath experienced by modern Witches is often presided over by a deity or deities, although it should be noted that this is not always the case, and for some practitioners there may be no deity involvement at all. If and when a deity or deities appear at the Sabbath, their specific identity will be contingent upon the individual Witch and who they have relationships with. Thus, one practitioner may find the Sabbath being led by Hecate while another may find Cernnunos fulfilling this role.

Within the practice of Traditional Witchcraft, many practitioners work with two archetypal beings referred to as the *Witch Father* and *Witch Mother*. The terms *father* and *mother* are not necessarily in reference to the pair as a duality or romantic/sexual companions, but they rather denote the pair's status as primordial beings from which all things originate. Therefore, these deities may appear together or separately at the Witches' Sabbath. Additionally, it's important to understand that these spirits, despite their monikers, are not inherently limited to any sort of gender binary and can easily move within the spectrum of masculine and feminine. In accordance with Witch Trial folklore, the Witch Father and Mother are also known as the Devil and the Queen of Elfame. The Devil in this case is not akin to the Christian concept of Satan but instead is a folkloric character often viewed as an amalgamation of various spirit beings lumped together by early persecutors. Among many things, the folkloric Devil is the embodiment of nature, both calm and chaotic at the same time. He is a shapeshifter capable of assuming many guises, a trickster who can be contradictory in his mysterious ways. Furthermore, he is both the Light Bringer who bestows life and the Lord of the Mound who heralds the dead. The Queen of Elfame is much the same, being both a creator and destroyer, breathing life into the world as well as laying out the bones of the dead. She is a magical initiator, revealing the art of Witchcraft to all those who seek its power. Furthermore, and perhaps above all else, she is the weaver of fate, spinning the very threads of destiny upon her wheel.

At the Witches' Sabbath, deities serve as the leaders and masters of ceremony, guiding attendees through magical workings and overseeing the wild revelries. In such a role, deities can be honored, gratitude expressed, and bonds strengthened. Furthermore, it's possible that new deities can be met with and fresh working relationships established. As per the folklore, deities at the Sabbath can provide powerful initiatory experiences—including awakening one to their very powers as a Witch. These profound rites of transformation can spark deep emotional and spiritual change within anyone who has the chance to undergo them. Additionally, like the stories of the Devil instructing Sabbath attendees in the use of spells and charms, deities act as advisors on the ways of the Craft. Through such interactions you might learn new skills or techniques for working your magical will—both to bless and to blast as seen fit.

Witches

In folklore, a major part of the Sabbath's company was made up of the Witches themselves. When attending the Sabbath today, you will thus find yourself among the spirit forms of many other Witches. The role of these Witches, like that of the folkloric coven, is to provide support and assistance in magical workings. Each Witch lends their strength and power to the spells or rituals at hand, creating a greater chance for success. It's also possible that these spirit Witches at the Sabbath can offer a sense of occult community connection and belonging, especially to those who are without such relationships in the waking world. In any case, having the aid of these Witches is invaluable and working alongside them can prove to be a considerably thrilling experience. But the question remains, who are these other Witches? Are they Witches from around the world? Are they the spirits of deceased Witches? Both could very well be true. For the most part, though, the other Witches at the Sabbath will be unrecognizable to you. Perhaps because of the Sabbath's innate secrecy, the true identity of attendees is obscured by some sort of enchantment.

That being said, it is possible that you might, on occasion, randomly see someone you know in the mundane world among the coven of Witches at the Sabbath. However, in my experience, I have found this to be pretty rare. You may try to synchronize journeying to the Sabbath with another Witch—or even a whole coven of Witches—in hopes of gathering together in the Otherworld. If you have the opportunity to practice with other Witches, this can be quite the feat to attempt! In order to do so, you and the other Witch(es) will need to coordinate the timing of your trip to Sabbath. For example, you might plan for the journey to commence at 9 p.m., at which time all participants would begin their ritual processes. Additionally, if there is a particular intention or goal for the Sabbath meeting, such as a specific magical working, all participants will need to be on the same page. Once at the Sabbath, you'll need to focus on the image of the other Witch or Witches with whom you're convening, calling out to their spirits. If successful, you will find each other and be able to engage in the Sabbath together. If you are unable to locate one another, don't be discouraged! Continue with your Sabbath journey as it naturally unfolds and try again another time. Furthermore, even if you are able to find your fellow Witches at the Sabbath, don't be surprised if you later discover that your experiences were still wildly varied.

Familiar Spirits

Today, the term *familiar* is popularly used by Witches to describe a physical-bodied pet who displays a particular magical curiosity. However, in keeping with folklore, Traditional Witches work with familiars as noncorporal, attending spirits. As noted in the previous chapter, the exact nature of familiar spirits can be difficult to determine. Are they faeries? Ghosts? Demons? The fact of the matter is that the term *familiar spirit* is more of an umbrella that covers a number of different eldritch beings, regardless of specific type, with whom Witches form intimate, working relationships. The bond between a Witch and their familiar can take on many forms, with the latter acting as a servant, friend, partner, or even teacher. And just as it is within folklore, a Witch can receive a familiar spirit in a miscellany of ways, including through the intercession of a deity or higher spirit, being passed on by or inherited from another practitioner, or the familiar showing up of their own volition. Additionally, it is also possible for a Witch to summon a familiar spirit through the use of certain spells or rituals (see pages 110–12 of my book *The Crooked Path*). If you are without a familiar spirit but desire to work with one, you very well might find one at the Sabbath.

By and large, the familiar spirit's role in regard to the Witches' Sabbath is as a guide or transport. While it may not be inherently necessary, having a familiar spirit to help you navigate your way through the Otherworld and to the Sabbath can be fairly advantageous. Like the Witches of folklore riding upon or alongside their familiars, modern practitioners can entreat their attending spirit to carry their spectral form through the night air and to the awaiting Sabbath ground. In order to do this, you would simply need to communicate your desire to your familiar spirit that you would like for them to help transport your spirit to an intended Otherworldly location, specifically the Witches' Sabbath. This can be done before engaging in spirit flight or after you have already crossed the hedge. Depending upon the guise your familiar spirit takes, you might proceed to ride upon their back or fly alongside them on some other implement, such as a broomstick or pitchfork.

The Fair Folk

At the Sabbath you may also encounter the Fair Folk, or faeries. Perhaps you will find yourself at a Faerie Sabbath proper. Regardless, it's vital to understand that these are not the faeries as popularly depicted today—

diminutive, gossamer-winged creatures of love and light. Instead, these are the same faeries as described in folklore. They come in many shapes and sizes and might very well look quite human, save a few Otherworldly tells such as outdated or whimsical clothing and a slight, unearthly glow. Additionally, it's absolutely imperative to be aware that the Fair Folk are amoral and are thus capable of both helping and harming humans as they see fit. This is not meant to scare you but rather caution you to take care when approaching a faerie, for they may not always have your best interest in mind. That being said, folklore does show Witches having a relationship with the Fair Folk that is considerably different from that between the common individual and faerie. And if you end up encountering faeries at the Witches' Sabbath, or even find yourself at a Faerie Sabbath, it's likely due to their interest in working with you. While it would still be advisable to tread lightly, I believe that this is a sign of beneficence on the part of the Fair Folk. I will discuss ways of safely engaging with spirits, including faeries, later in this chapter.

Faeries at the Sabbath function much like the other Witches, providing magical assistance in spellwork and ritual. As they are naturally talented with enchantments and glamours, these are particular areas in which faeries may lend assistance at the Sabbath. In addition to working magic, the Fair Folk provide much in the way of celebration at the Sabbath, including charming music and lively dancing. Although, be aware that folklore has warned against eating or drinking anything given to you by a faerie, as it is believed to instantly trap you into their servitude. While Witches may have a better footing with the Fair Folk than most, I still wouldn't risk my personal autonomy by joining their feasting table.

Ancestors

Although they rarely feature in folklore, other spirits you may encounter at the Witches' Sabbath are ancestral spirits. Ancestors are the spirits of deceased humans, specifically those with whom we shared some sort of relationship. When we think of ancestral spirits, we most often think about those individuals with whom we shared a biological connection, such as grandparents, great-grandparents, and so on, stretching far back into the unknown depths of history. However, this is not the only type of ancestral spirit, and it is not necessary to share blood in order to be considered such. Take, for example, the importance of an adopted or chosen family. Additionally, we have land-based ancestors, or the spirits of the people who lived on your land before you. For Witches, we also consider the Mighty Dead, or the spirits of other magical practitioners who have passed beyond the veil. In regard to the Sabbath, the other Witches encountered there may in fact be members of the Mighty Dead. There are many other types of ancestral spirits, beyond the scope of what can be covered here. If you don't know the specific names of your ancestors, that is okay too! You might simply refer to them as "ancestors unknown" when communicating. Furthermore, if you have problematic ancestors you don't wish to engage with, you need not and can instead focus your attention elsewhere.

Our ancestors, whether familial, land-based, or spiritual, are keepers of ancient wisdom. They are stewards of history and lore, links in a chain that spans both backward and forward in time. Like all other types of spirits, we have the ability to connect and communicate with our ancestors anytime, anywhere. Yet we have greater access to them while in the Otherworld and even more so at the Witches' Sabbath. There are numerous ways in which you might engage with your ancestors while at the Sabbath, including getting to know unknown members of your family tree, working to heal intergenerational trauma, obtaining blessings and protection, and giving reverence and honor.

Engaging with the Spirits of the Sabbath

It is inevitable that you will encounter spirits, whatever type they may be, at the Sabbath. After all, developing meaningful relationships with different spirits is one of the main purposes for these Otherworldly convocations. The first thing to know when going about establishing relationships with spirits is that it's a process not unlike what we go through when meeting new people in the physical world. As such, engaging with spirits need not be overly complicated but it should be done with mindfulness and respect. As off-putting as it might be, it's crucial to know that not all spirits will have your best interests in mind. Many spirits harbor beneficent feelings toward humankind, but others can be ambivalent or even hostile. That being said, personal safety while meeting with spirits can be bolstered by having a thorough knowledge and understanding of them and of yourself.

Knowing Them

First and foremost, it's vital to know about the type of spirit with whom you are interacting. Are they a deity, a familiar, or an ancestor? Are they perhaps a different type of spirit not discussed within the pages of this book? Even within a given category of spirit type, there are many different sub-categories. For example, there are several types of faeries, and they each have their own unique personality traits and magical virtues. To gain this knowledge, it's important to do your research. Read books on different Otherworldly beings (see the recommended reading and bibliography at the end of this book), including compendiums of spirits, folklore anthologies, and even fairy tales. Pay attention to the temperament of each spirit, their quirks, their likes and dislikes, and their general attitude toward humans. Additionally, understand that each type of spirit often has their own cultural dos and don'ts. Knowing the proper mannerisms to use when approaching certain types of spirits can prevent you from pissing them off and potentially landing yourself in a dangerous position. Of course, there will also be spirits who, for whatever reason, will not want to confer with you. While their presence at the Sabbath is a good indicator that a spirit is interested in you, this may not always be the case. Regardless of their reasoning, it's advisable that you respect their boundaries and move on.

Knowing Yourself

At the same time that it's pertinent to have knowledge about the spirits you might encounter at the Sabbath, it's important to know yourself. Specifically, it's necessary to be honest with yourself regarding your skill level.

When you are new to working with spirits, it's prudent to take it slow. Don't approach or attempt to work with spirits you do not know about or those whom you are not entirely comfortable with. While there is much to be said about challenging oneself and stepping outside your comfort zone, it's also good practice to know and respect your limits. There is no use in rushing into something that you are not prepared for. Furthermore, if a spirit approaches you, know that you are not automatically obliged to respond to them. Even though respect should always be considered, if a spirit approaches you and you get a bad feeling, it's entirely valid to turn the other way. The same goes if a spirit makes a request of you that you find to be inappropriate or dangerous. In these cases, it is completely acceptable to politely, yet firmly, ask the spirit to back off. If you are unsure of a spirit's intentions, it's okay to ask them or even challenge them. For example, if a spirit expresses that they want to help you in some way but the offer seems sketchy, it's all right to ask them for specific details and to say no if you find their answers unacceptable. Finally, depending upon the type of spirit, if they are not respectful of your boundaries, you may need to either banish them (see the following exercise) or leave the Sabbath by returning to your axis mundi.

 EXERCISE
Banishing a Spirit from the Sabbath

The following method can be used while at the Sabbath in order to banish an unruly spirit. This method should be employed as a last resort or in extreme cases only, as it can both disrupt the overall journey and create relational disturbances with the other spirits present. Luckily, there is typically very little need to banish a spirit from the Sabbath.

To begin, take a step back from the spirit you are about to banish. Take a deep breath in and feel the magical power swirling in your core. Extend your left hand and quickly draw a banishing pentagram in the space between you and the spirit. Then, pull the magical energy up from your core and project it out through your hands (both arms extended outward, palms open and flat)—envisioning it as a brilliantly colored light. Allow the light to dissolve the spirit's form, effectively banishing their presence. When you feel the spirit has gone, visualize the light receding back into your palms. Finish by drawing an additional banishing pentagram in the air:

 EXERCISE
Creating a Protective Charm Bag

Another way to keep yourself safe while at the Sabbath and in the Otherworld in general is to craft a protective charm bag.

Necessary Items
Small square of dark blue cloth
Mugwort
Mullein
Cedar bark
Black-colored stone
Red marker or pen
Small piece of parchment paper
Disposable lancet (optional)
Length of red thread

Begin by laying out the small square of blue cloth. Take a pinch of mugwort and ask for its assistance in protecting your spiritual body from harm. Place the mugwort atop the cloth. Next, take a pinch of mullein and ask for its assistance in providing clear sight, to help spot any possible dangers around you while on your journey. Add the mullein to the mugwort atop the cloth. Take a pinch of cedar and ask for its assistance in guarding you from any malevolent spirits. Add the cedar to the mugwort and mullein atop the cloth. Moving forward, hold the black-colored stone in your hand and ask for its assistance in providing a protective barrier around your spirit while it moves through the Otherworld and upon the Sabbath ground. Then, using the red marker or pen, copy the following sigil onto the piece of parchment paper. This sigil invokes protection at the Sabbath, combining symbols for the Upperworld, Midworld, and Underworld, along with the runes Raido and Algiz.

Take the lancet and procure a drop of blood from your left thumb, pressing it into the center of the pentagram, thus sealing the sigil with your essence. If you are unable to or uncomfortable with using blood, lick your left thumb and mark the sigil with your saliva. Finally, fold up the parchment and add it to herbs and stone atop the cloth.

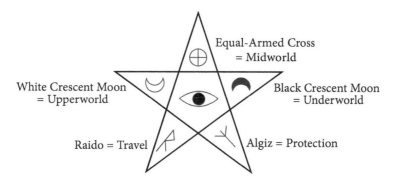

Finish the amulet by pulling up the corners of the cloth and tying it together with the red thread. Leave enough thread so that you can wear the charm bag around your neck. Tie three knots for extra power. Hold the finished amulet in your hands and feel the virtues of the herbs, stone, cloth, thread, paper, and ink melding together and merging with your own magical power. When you feel that the protective energies have aligned, recite the following spell:

Around my neck, a magic charm
To keep my spirit safe from harm,
Bound together by knot of three.
Safe at the Sabbath, I shall be.

⬠ EXERCISE
Calling a Spirit to the Witches' Sabbath

If there is a particular spirit with whom you'd like to meet at the Sabbath, this simple invocation can be used to encourage their presence. Please note that this spell is meant for *encouraging* not *forcing* a spirit to appear. There are many reasons why a spirit might not attend a given Sabbath gathering, and it's important to respect their autonomy. If you use this spell and find that the spirit or spirits don't show, you'll just have to wait for another time and try again.

Attempting to coerce a spirit to meet with you is both foolish and severely damaging to your relationship.

The following spell should be spoken before crossing the hedge into the Otherworld, allowing time for the spirit to receive your invitation. In your mind's eye, conjure the image of the spirit, paying attention to the fine details of their appearance. Once you have fully pictured the spirit, speak the following invocation thrice while focusing on the words floating like smoke into the Otherworld, where they will be received by your intended target.

> *Across the sky, the land, and sea,*
> *(Spirit), hear my call to thee.*
> *I invoke your name; please come around*
> *To meet with me at the Sabbath ground!*

Once finished, you may then move on to your other Sabbath preparations (which will be discussed fully in chapter 8).

Chapter 7
WICKED RITES
AND DEBAUCHED REVELRIES

Now that we have a feel for where the Sabbath is located, how to travel there, and who we'll be gathering with, it's time for us to take one last trip into the past in order to examine the folklore regarding what events took place therein. From the infamous Black Mass to spirited ring dances, the Sabbath folklore included acts of both business and pleasure. Typically, meetings were organized into two distinct halves, with business coming before pleasure or vice versa. However, there are also some accounts of Sabbaths featuring only one or the other. Regardless, activities at the Sabbath were performed in order to carry out the Devil's agenda, which was to fortify his presence on earth as well as to sow discord and chaos. To that end, he was most interested in using the Sabbath as a time to recruit new Witches, receive homage, and to incite blasphemy. Additionally, as noted previously, the Devil actively taught Witches how to make use of malefica. Despite the fact that he sometimes forcefully encouraged the perpetuation of wicked actions, Witches were often capable and more than willing to use such skills to achieve their own mischievous intentions.

Aside from the more somber matters of business, accounts of the Sabbath often sounded a lot like rambunctious community festivals. In fact, it is quite likely that in order to satisfy their interrogators, many of the accused augmented their confessions by repurposing memories of mundane celebratory gatherings they had attended in the past. As such, the more carnivalesque aspects of the Witches' Sabbath included feasting, dancing, and music making, as well as sexual congress. While this merrymaking was frequently stained by the inclusion of diabolical acts (e.g., cannibalism and incest), it also contained a deep, underlying sense of freedom as Witches effectively subverted the repressive standards of Christian society. And by engaging in pleasurable activities, Witches also shed the many stressors of their mundane lives and traded them in for a night of enchantment and folly.

Initiation

Above all else, the Devil was widely believed to enjoy nothing more than corrupting the human population, to lead them away from God's light. For this reason, the Devil officiated certain rituals through which individuals stripped themselves of their previous Christian faith and took on the mantle of Witch. The motivations such people had for choosing to align with the Devil often reflected the everyday struggles that they faced. For example, Jeanette Clerc explained how the Devil had guaranteed her all the money she could want in exchange for allegiance.[193] Niclas Fiedler was assured that his sick wife would recover.[194] Mary Toothaker was promised she would be safe from Indian attacks.[195] Margaret Johnson was told that she would have vengeance upon anyone she so desired.[196] Whether it was to attain money, health, protection, or justice, many reasons for becoming a Witch were cited within trial transcripts. While rituals of initiation were frequently a part of the Sabbath, they were also at times required before a Witch was allowed to attend. In either case,

---

193. Monter, *Witchcraft in France and Switzerland*, 56.

194. "The Confession of Niclas Fiedler at Trier, 1591," in *The Witchcraft Sourcebook*, ed. Brian P. Levack (London: Routledge, 2015), 200.

195. "SWP No. 128: Mary Toothaker," Salem Witch Trials Documentary Archive and Transcription Project, accessed February 5, 2021, http://salem.lib.virginia.edu/n128 .html.

196. Harland and Wilkinson, *Lancashire Folk-Lore*, 193.

these rites of induction commonly included one or more of the following components: the renunciation of the Christian God, an oath of fidelity, and a baptism during which the initiate was given a special mark and a new name.

Renunciations of Faith

In order for a new Witch to be received by the Devil, they first had to wholeheartedly renounce Christianity. As an act of apostasy, the renunciation was typically expressed verbally in the presence of the Devil as well as the other Witches present. At minimum, the initiate would renounce the Christian God, such as Isabel Becquet who confessed that she knelt before the Devil and said, "I renounce God the Father, God the Son, and God the Holy Ghost."[197] Similarly, Johannes Junius of Bamberg, Germany, confessed in 1628 that he had spoken the following: "I renounce God in Heaven and his host, and will henceforth recognize the Devil as my God." He noted that afterward, the other Witches present congratulated him in Beelzebub's name and commented that they were now all alike.[198] In other cases, though, Witches renounced several Christian spirits during their initiation. For example, Wawrzyniec Dziad of Jarocin, Poland, confessed in 1719 that he had renounced God, the Virgin Mary, and all the saints.[199]

Verbal Oaths and Written Pacts

After renouncing their previous beliefs, the new Witches were required to pledge their allegiance to the Devil, who from that point forward would be their master. Like the renunciation, oaths were often given through verbal expression. Walpurga Hausmännin confessed that she had knelt

---

197. "The Confessions of Witches in Guernsey, 1617," in *The Witchcraft Sourcebook*, 210–11.

198. "The Confessions of Johannes Junius at Bamberg, 1628," in *The Witchcraft Sourcebook*, ed. Brian P. Levack (London: Routledge, 2015), 215–16.

199. Wyporska, *Witchcraft in Early Modern Poland 1500–1800*, 61.

before the Devil and dedicated herself, body and soul, to him.[200] Other times, a written pact was required, although this was much more common in situations where the Devil appeared to a would-be Witch outside of the Sabbath. However, the Witches in Mora, Sweden, confessed to having made both a verbal and written pact with the Devil while at Blåkulla. In this case, initiates cut their fingers and used the blood to write their names in his book. They were then given a small pouch containing the "filings of a clock," which they threw into a nearby source of water while repeating the following words: "As these filings of the Clock do never return to the Clock from which they are taken, so may my Soul never return to Heaven."[201]

Infernal Baptisms, Devil's Marks, and Witch's Names

Besides renunciations and oaths, some initiation rituals also featured a sort of dark baptism through which the initiate formally received their new identity as a Witch. In some instances, such baptisms directly parodied the Church. For example, Mary Osgood of Andover, Massachusetts, confessed in 1692 that she had flown with three other Witches to a pond where the Devil dipped her face in the water and rebaptized her.[202] To further signify their transition, the new Witches were often given a special mark upon their body. Written in 1645 by the nom de plume "Authority," *The Lawes against VVitches, and Conivration* described how "the Devil leaveth other markes upon their bodies, sometimes like a Blew-spot, or

---

200. "The Confessions of Walpurga Hausmännin, 1587," in *The Witchcraft Sourcebook*, ed. Brian P. Levack (London: Routledge, 2015), 194.

201. Anthony Horneck, "An Account of What Happened in the Kingdom of Sweden in the Years 1669, and 1670," in Glanvill, *Saducismus Triumphatus*, 321–22. As pointed out to me by Val Thomas, the Swedish word *klocka* can mean both "clock" and "bell." Given that Swedish folklore often mentions Witches scraping metal filings from church bells for various purposes, it's more than likely that Horneck mistranslated the word here.

202. "SWP No. 096: Mary Osgood," Salem Witch Trials Documentary Archive and Transcription Project, accessed February 5, 2021, http://salem.lib.virginia.edu/n96.html.

Red-spot, like a flea-biting, sometimes the flesh sunck in and hollow."[203] These marks were typically created by the Devil biting some area of the Witch's body. For example, Jeanette Clerc claimed that she was given her mark when the Devil bit the right side of her face.[204] Furthermore, the initiate was often given a new name to replace the one they had received during their Christian baptism. This practice was particularly popular in Scotland but was also found in other countries as well. For example, in Germany, Walpurga Hausmännin confessed that during her initiation she was rebaptized and given the new name of Höfelin.[205]

An illustrious account of an initiation that incorporated all three customs—renunciation, oath making, and baptism—comes from the confessions of Isobel Gowdie. According to her story, Gowdie met with the Devil and other Witches during the night at a church in Auldearn. Upon arriving, she first denied her Christian baptism. Then, crouching down, she placed one hand atop her head and the other beneath the soles of her feet. In this position she promised everything between her two hands to the Devil. Next, a coven member named Margaret Brodie presented Gowdie to the Devil for her infernal baptism. For this, the Devil marked Gowdie on the shoulder and sucked out some of her blood. He spit the blood into his hand and then sprinkled it over her head, proclaiming, "I baptize thee Janet!"[206]

Blasphemy and the Black Mass

Acts of blasphemy were typical among the more formal tasks completed by Witches at the Sabbath. Such acts not only proved a Witch's allegiance to the Devil but also helped strengthen his powers on earth. Blasphemous deeds included cursing the names of Christian spirits and

---

203. Authority, *The Lawes against VVitches, and Conivration* (London: R. W., 1645; Ann Arbor, MI: Text Creation Partnership, 2011), 4.

204. Monter, *Witchcraft in France and Switzerland*, 56–57.

205. "The Confessions of Walpurga Hausmännin, 1587," in *The Witchcraft Sourcebook*, 193–95.

206. Pitcairn, *Ancient Criminal Trials in Scotland*, vol. 3, 603.

purposefully reciting prayers incorrectly as well as the desecration of holy objects. For example, Anne Armstrong reported that she sat around a stone with a number of other Witches and bent forward while reciting the Lord's Prayer backward.[207] Walpurga Hausmännin and those present at her meeting took to tramping the holy sacrament as well as an image of the holy cross.[208] At times, more ceremonial acts of blasphemy were accounted for, specifically those that parodied the rituals of the Catholic Church. Popularly known as a *Black Mass*, these ceremonies involved the inversion of Christian elements. On the subject, Boguet wrote that, "Sometimes, again, they [Witches] say Mass at the Sabbat. But I cannot write without horror of the manner in which it is celebrated."[209] The appearance of these Black Masses in Sabbath narratives was most common in countries that were closer to the Holy Roman Empire. As such, one of the most descriptive accounts of a Black Mass at the Sabbath comes from the accounts of those accused of Witchcraft in Spain.

According to the accused Spanish Witches, they placed upon an altar images of the Devil as well as a chalice, host, missal, cruets, and vestments, which were described as being ugly, black, and dirty. The Devil gave a sermon in which he decreed that the Witches were not to acknowledge any god other than himself. He assured the Witches that he would be the one to save and deliver them to paradise. Furthermore, he stated that although the Witches would go through hard times, in the afterlife he would grant them repose. Alms were then given, including bread and eggs, before the Witches kissed the Devil's left hand, breasts, private parts, and behind. Next, the Devil elevated "something around like the sole of a shoe," upon which was painted an image of his face. During this time, the coven chanted "*Aquerragoiti, aquerrabeiti,*" or "Up with the he-goat, down with the he-goat." Finally, communion was administered, consisting of a black

---

207. Hole, *Witchcraft in England,* 125.
208. "The Confessions of Walpurga Hausmännin, 1587," 195.
209. Boguet, *An Examen of Witches,* 60.

morsel that was very dry and hard to swallow as well as a draft of a very bitter drink that chilled the Witches' hearts.[210]

Malefica

In addition to the rites of initiation and acts of blasphemy, the Sabbath was also a dedicated time for the working of malefica. The unnamed woman from Eichstätt confessed that at the Sabbath, the Witches not only blasphemed the Christian God, but they also plotted how to commit harmful acts of magic.[211] In many cases, Witches were required to report to the Devil the destruction that they had wrought since the meeting prior. For instance, Agnes Sampson confessed that at the start of her meeting, the Devil demanded whether the Witches had kept their promises and been good servants, asking specifically what acts of malevolence they had committed since they had last convened.[212] During these recountings, any Witch who was found to be slacking in their duties was punished accordingly. Remy noted in his writing that the Devil "terribly vents his wrath upon those who cannot show proof that they have gone on increasing in crimes and wickedness."[213] Boguet explained further that those Witches who seemingly shirked their responsibilities were often verbally and physically abused by the Devil as well as the other coven members.[214] Broadly speaking, the malefica enacted at the Sabbath can be broken down into two categories: harm to humans and livestock and the destruction of crops and material goods.

Harm to Humans and Livestock

Within folklore, harm to humans and livestock stood as one of the hallmarks of a Witch's power, and it was one of the popularly cited Sabbath

---

210. Frías, "An Account of the Persons at the Auto de Fe," in *The Salazar Documents,* 120–22.

211. "The Witch-Hunt at Eichstätt," in *The Witchcraft Sourcebook,* 224.

212. Pitcairn, *Ancient Criminal Trials in Scotland,* vol. 1, 239.

213. Remy, *Demonolatry,* 68.

214. Boguet, *An Examen of Witches,* 59.

activities. For example, Margaret Johnson confessed that she and the other Witches present at the Sabbath consulted on the hurting and killing of both men and beasts.[215] In many cases, the individual who became the recipient of malefica was someone who had been deemed an enemy, either by the Devil or one of the Witches. In order to smite their adversaries, Witches would either target these individuals directly or indirectly by attacking their family members and livestock. The harm induced by Witches could range anywhere from illness to death and was often accomplished through the implementation of poisonous powders and ointments as well as dolls or other images created in the likeness of their victim.

The creation and exchange of poisonous powders and ointments was a common occurrence at the Sabbath and harkens back to the early accusations lobbied against lepers and Jews. These toxic substances were crafted so that Witches would be able to use them to harm others—victims who were chosen either by the Devil or at the Witch's own discretion. An early recipe for such poisons can be found in the *Errores gazariorum*, which described an ointment made from the fat of children along with snakes, toads, lizards, and spiders. The author noted that if anyone were unfortunate enough to touch this ointment, they would die a most painful death for which there was no remedy.[216] In Guernsey, Collette Du Mont confessed that at the Sabbath, the Devil encouraged her to commit different evil acts and gave her a black powder that she could throw upon people and cattle—presumably in order to make them ill or even die.[217] A French woman named Marie d'Aspilcoutte confessed that the Witches in her coven would rub their hands with a green ointment, after which anyone they touched would die or fall bewitched and miserable for the rest of their lives. D'Aspilcoutte noted that this ointment was so toxic that the Witches had to wash their hands with a special water within two to three

---

215. Harland and Wilkinson, *Lancashire Folk-Lore*, 198.

216. Anonymous, "The Errores Gazariorum," in *Witchcraft in Europe: 400–1700*, ed. Alan Charles Kors and Edward Peters (Philadelphia: University of Pennsylvania, 2001), 161.

217. "The Confessions of Witches in Guernsey, 1617," in *The Witchcraft Sourcebook*, 211.

hours or they too would suffer.[218] Similarly, two accused Witches, Madeleine Merlou and Anthonia Preudhon from Peseux, Switzerland, confessed in 1583 that at the Sabbath the Devil had given them some herbs with which they created a poisonous grease. Said grease was then rubbed onto windows and doors so that anyone unlucky enough to touch them would become sick and die.[219]

Another method through which harm could be magically administered, to humans specifically, was through the use of *poppets*—images created to represent a certain person. It was thought that harm inflicted to the poppet would also then manifest upon the intended target. In order to inflict harm, the poppets were commonly stuck with sharp objects, such as pins or thorns, or slowly roasted over a fire. These images were sometimes supplied by the Devil, while other times they were handed out by other Witches. As such, it was said that at the Witch meeting in Salem, George Burroughs provided the other Witches with poppets and thorns to stick them with in order to afflict other people.[220] Additionally, some Witches even brought premade poppets to the Sabbath in order to have them empowered by the Devil. For example, Elizabeth Style reported that Alice Duke had brought an image made of wax to the Sabbath. The Man in Black took it from her and anointed the doll's forehead, saying, "I Baptize thee with this Oyl." The coven members then proceeded to stick the image with thorns, pricking the neck, wrists, fingers, and other parts. Further on in her confession, Style notes that when her coven would use such images, they would sometimes say the words, "A pox on thee, I'le spite thee."[221]

---

218. De Lancre, *On the Inconstancy of Witches*, 150.

219. Monter, *Witchcraft in France and Switzerland*, 94.

220. Cotton Mather, "Wonders of the Invisible World," in *Narratives of the New England Witchcraft Cases*, ed. George Lincoln Burr (Mineola, NY: Dover Publications, 2012), 219.

221. Glanvill, *Saducismus Triumphatus*, 139.

Destruction of Crops and Material Goods

Secondary to the harm of humans and livestock, the magical destruction of crops and other material goods (especially milk, beer, and wine) was also a routine form of malefica performed at the Sabbath. For instance, Niclas Fiedler confessed that he, along with others who had been present at the Sabbath, had plotted to destroy the local wine and grain harvests.[222] This particular form of malefica was especially important because laying waste to another's field or spoiling their goods meant quite literally obliterating their livelihood and quite possibly decreasing their chances of survival due to resulting poverty and starvation. Thus, another powerful way for a Witch to cause harm to an enemy would be to target their crops and material goods. Although, in some regions it would seem that this destruction was done more at the behest of the Devil and less on account of the Witches' own agenda. For example, in France, where covens were often thought to be composed of Witches from differing socioeconomic classes, those who were poor often bemoaned the Devil's orders to ruin crops due to a fear that their own fields would be ruined in the process. Thus, Claudette Delat confessed in 1608 that she begged the Devil to spare the grain because she was poor and worried that she would go hungry as a result of the destruction.[223]

Methods through which crop destruction was achieved were highly varied across regions, but they tended to include contamination as well as the conjuration of foul weather. The former modus operandi typically required the use of noxious substances, bodily fluids, or poisons being spread over fields or added to material goods. As an example, an accused Polish Witch named Marusza Staszkowa confessed that he was taught how to use horse ashes to ruin beer.[224] The accused Spanish Witches reportedly concocted powders made from toads, snakes, lizards, slugs, snails, and puffballs. They were said to take this powder to the highest peaks, where they would scat-

---

222. "The Confession of Niclas Fiedler at Trier, 1591," in *The Witchcraft Sourcebook*, 201.
223. Briggs, *The Witches of Lorraine*, 138.
224. Wyporska, *Witchcraft in Early Modern Poland 1500–1800*, 183.

ter it over the crops, tossing it over their shoulders with their left hands while the Devil implored, "May all be lost!" The Witches would repeat these words, adding, "May mine be saved!"[225] In regard to foul weather, Witches were believed to have the ability to summon unfavorable conditions, especially hail. Niclas Fiedler commented in his confession that the women in his coven knew how to destroy corn by summoning a storm, which they did by beating on the surface of a stream in the Devil's name.[226] Additionally, Marie d'Aspilcoutte mentioned how her coven would throw a specially made powder into the mist that came in from the sea or down from the mountains. The powder would mix with the clouds and turn into a fog or rain that would then ruin local crops.[227]

However, while fields were often blighted, this form of malefica was not limited to total devastation. Remy noted that among the malefica the Devil taught to Witches was the skill of charming the crops away from another's field.[228] Again adding more detail, Boguet explained how "it is said that witches, with the help of their Master, strip the fruit from one field and cause it to be transferred to another."[229] A prime example comes from the confession of Isobel Gowdie who explained how her coven performed a ritual in which a plow, driven by frogs, was used to steal the crops from a field, leaving nothing but thistles and briars in their place.[230] Additionally, Gowdie detailed a method used by her coven to steal the milk from cows by braiding the cow's tail the "vrong way" (likely left hand over right) and pulling it forward between the back legs and out between the front ones.[231] And, as noted earlier, Witches were not above breaking into the homes of sleeping people in order to steal from their store of food and drink.

---

225. Frías, "An Account of the Persons at the Auto de Fe," in *The Salazar Documents*, 126.

226. "The Confession of Niclas Fiedler at Trier, 1591," in *The Witchcraft Sourcebook*, 202.

227. De Lancre, *On the Inconstancy of Witches*, 150.

228. Remy, *Demonolatry*, 68.

229. Boguet, *An Examen of Witches*, 97.

230. Pitcairn, *Ancient Criminal Trials in Scotland*, vol. 3, 603.

231. Pitcairn, *Ancient Criminal Trials in Scotland*, vol. 3, 605.

Feasting

The Sabbath often included a feast of sorts, whether it was in the form of a full-fledged banquet or a simple meal shared among a few Witches. During times when many people struggled to meet their needs, these Otherworldly suppers perhaps represented a fantasy of nutritional fulfillment. Feasting often took place toward the end of the Sabbath, although this was not a hard-and-fast rule. In one case, Ann Foster confessed that the Witches of her coven had a picnic under a tree before their meeting.[232] During the meal, the Devil was always seated at the head of the table. Again, it was common that one woman from the coven would be selected to sit next to him, usually on the basis of her beauty or prowess as a Witch. At times, a prayer would be given by one of the Witches or the Devil himself before they ate. Isobel Gowdie provided a complete example of such a blessing, explaining how Alexander Elder was chosen to say grace before they ate:

> We eat this meat in The Divellis nam,
> With sorrow, and sych, and meikle shame;
> We sall destroy hows and hald;
> Both sheip and noat in till the fald.
> Litle good sall come to the for
> Of all the rest of the little store![233]

The food and drink at the Sabbath were often provided in one of two ways. First, the meal could be supplied by the Devil himself. Such was the case at one of the Sabbaths attended by Elizabeth Style, who confessed that the Man in Black gave the coven wine, cakes, and roast meat to eat.[234] Second, Witches could bring the food and drink themselves, either taken from their own supply or stolen from their neighbors. For example,

---

232. John Hale, "Modest Inquiry into the Nature of Witchcraft," in *Narratives of the New England Witchcraft Cases*, ed. George Lincoln Burr (Mineola, NY: Dover Publications, 2012), 418.

233. Pitcairn, *Ancient Criminal Trials in Scotland*, vol. 3, 612.

234. Glanvill, *Saducismus Triumphatus*, 138.

Ann Foster confessed that when going to her meeting, she brought bread and cheese from home, which she carried in her pocket.[235] Meanwhile, Helen Guthrie recounted how some of her coven members brought ale to the Sabbath that they had stolen from a local brewer.[236] Regardless of how it was obtained, the food and drink at the Sabbath varied widely both in content and in taste—ranging from delicious to disgusting. On one hand, the meal was sometimes described as rather ordinary or even quite scrumptious. For example, Anne Armstrong testified that the victuals at her meeting consisted of boiled capons, beef, butter, cheese, and wine.[237] The accused Witches of Mora, Sweden, had a feast consisting of broth with coleworts and bacon served alongside oatmeal, bread spread with butter, cheese, and milk.[238]

On the other hand, in some instances the food and drink were said to be unappetizing and even physically difficult to consume. This was particularly true when the Devil prepared the feast. Nicolas Remy stated that "all who have been honored at his [the Devil's] table confess that his banquets are so foul either in appearance or smell that they would easily cause nausea in the hungriest and greediest stomach."[239] The distasteful nature of the meal was often due to it being ill-prepared or because it consisted of noxious items. For example, an accused Polish woman named Anna Jasińska confessed that at the Sabbath they simply ate horse droppings and drank horse urine.[240] The unnamed Witch from Eichstätt reported that there was lots to eat and drink at the Sabbath, including roasts and stews served in green dishes. However, she noted the food was insipid, moldy, completely black, very sweet, indistinguishable, and ill-prepared.[241]

---

235. Hale, "Modest Inquiry Into the Nature of Witchcraft," 418.

236. Kinloch, *Reliquiae Antiquae Scoticae*, 121.

237. Hole, *Witchcraft in England*, 124–25.

238. Horneck, "An Account of What Happened in the Kingdom of Sweden in the Years 1669, and 1670," in Glanvill, *Saducismus Triumphatus*, 322.

239. Remy, *Demonolatry*, 57.

240. Wyporska, *Witchcraft in Early Modern Poland 1500–1800*, 39.

241. "The Witch-Hunt at Eichstätt," in *The Witchcraft Sourcebook*, 223.

In addition to food that tasted bland or sickening, it was also said that the Sabbath meal would never truly satisfy the Witches' hunger nor thirst. Remy noted that Witches always left the table as hungry as when they went to it. In fact, he believed that the feast was nothing more than a dream or an illusion.[242] French woman Clauda Vuillat confessed that her coven ate nothing but the wind at the Sabbath.[243] De Lancre wrote that "if anyone wanted to reach for the good meat, he touched nothing solid and found nothing but air."[244] He later hypothesized that the Sabbath meal's unsatisfactory or illusionary nature was actually caused by God, who did not want the food to act as temptation for humans.[245] As a further example of the animosity between God and the Devil, the latter would not allow salt at the Sabbath table. Boguet explains that this was because of the Devil's hatred toward all things holy, as salt was a common component used in baptismal rites. Additionally, he hypothesized that because salt was seen as symbolic of wisdom, God himself would not allow it at the Sabbath as a way of showing the Witches that their sinful actions were, above all else, incredibly foolish.[246]

Cannibalism

Taking a significantly darker turn, the Sabbath feast was sometimes said to entail the cooking and consumption of human flesh. In these cases, Witches were believed to enjoy a nightmarish buffet consisting of unbaptized babies and bodily remains that had been stolen from recently dug graves. The inclusion of cannibalism in the Sabbath narrative is not surprising considering its early development. Recall the fact that cannibalism was among the accusations faced by various groups of people—including heretical sects that would later become associated with Witchcraft. Additionally, as demonstrated with the striges, the cannibalistic Witch had

---

242. Remy, *Demonolatry*, 59.

243. Boguet, *An Examen of Witches*, 58–59.

244. De Lancre, *On the Inconstancy of Witches*, 211.

245. De Lancre, *On the Inconstancy of Witches*, 214.

246. Boguet, *An Examen of Witches*, 58.

already been a well-established trope in mythology and folklore. Thus, it was likely via these two channels that themes of cannibalism found their way into accounts of the Sabbath. However, while mentions of cannibalism were by no means rare, they were infrequent.

Of the popular writers on the subject of Witchcraft, most only made brief mentions of Witches dining on human body parts—especially in comparison to the length at which they discussed other matters. For instance, Nicolas Remy made a rather quick mention of a woman named Dominique Isabelle who confessed in 1583 that the tables at the Sabbath were sometimes laid with human flesh.[247] Even Heinrich Kramer made little mention of cannibalism in the *Malleus Maleficarum*. On the subject he wrote that "certain witches, against the instinct of human nature, and indeed against the nature of all beasts, with the possible exception of wolves, are in the habit of devouring and eating infant children." He then cited the story of the Inquisitor of Como, who claimed to have been summoned by the inhabitants of the County of Barby after a man discovered his child being killed and devoured by a group of women during the night.[248] There were also accounts of Sabbath feasting penned by other writers, such as Henry Boguet and Jean Bodin, in which acts of cannibalism were entirely absent.

In a rare instance, cannibalism found its way into a Scottish confession when Helen Guthrie admitted that she, along with the other members of her coven, devoured an unbaptized baby. Interestingly, Guthrie explained that this was done in order that none of the coven members would ever be able to confess to their Witchery—an act reminiscent of the idea that heretical sects would trick initiates into acts of infanticide as a way to ensure their fealty.[249] However, it's the stories from the Basque region that offer us the most information regarding cannibalism at the Witches' Sabbath. On the French side, Pierre de Lancre reported that the majority of

---

247. Remy, *Demonolatry*, 58.

248. Kramer and Sprenger, *The Malleus Maleficarum*, 66.

249. Kinloch, *Reliquiae Antiquae Scoticae*, 121.

accused Witches he heard from confessed that among the many unsightly things consumed at their assemblies were the flesh of people who had recently been hanged, that of corpses from freshly dug graves, and that which belonged to unbaptized babies. De Lancre also provided a rare, detailed account of Sabbath cannibalism given by Jeanette d'Abadie, who recalled how she had seen many baptized and unbaptized children being eaten. In particular she commented on how she witnessed a child's ear being eaten by a Witch named Marie Balcoin. D'Abadie further explained that Witches never ate a whole child at a Sabbath held in one individual parish. Thus, a child she saw cut into pieces was divided up—one piece being consumed at the meeting and three other pieces being sent off to different parishes.[250]

In an odd twist, the accused Witches on the Spanish side of the Basque region were said to consume the bodies of their recently deceased coven members. Before leaving for the akelarre, the Witches would go along with the Devil to the local cemetery. There, with hoes in hand, the Witches would disinter the corpses of their former compatriots. Once they were well stocked, the Witches would depart for their Sabbath meeting, at which they ate the collected flesh roasted, boiled, or raw—reporting that it tasted more flavorsome than any other food they had ever eaten. It was noted, though, that any hearts procured from the grave were always given to the Devil because they were the tastiest of all the body parts. The Witches also gave portions of the flesh to their toad familiars, which they were said to eat "doggedly." Afterward, the Witches would gather any leftovers and bring them home—keeping them with their supply of bread and wine. These leftovers could be consumed at any time and the taste would be no less delicious than it had been at the akelarre.[251]

---

250. De Lancre, *On the Inconstancy of Witches*, 211–12.

251. Wilby, *Invoking the Akelarre*, 208–9.

Dancing

Alongside the feasting, Witches also enjoyed dancing about the Sabbath ground. These dances were described as being wild, rambunctious affairs that could be both lively and entertaining or dreadful and painfully exhausting. Remy wrote that "those dancings and caperings, which are ordinarily a pleasure, never fail to cause weariness and fatigue and the greatest distress." He goes on to explain how Barbelina Rayel confessed in 1587 that upon returning home from the Sabbath she was so tired that she had to lie down for two days in order to recover from the dancing.[252] On the other hand, De Lancre purported that at the nocturnal meetings, Witches danced with joy and ease—particularly the "lame, crippled, and old decrepit and the almost dead."[253] In either case, the dances were a boisterous matter that quickly devolved into a frenzy. For example, Waldburga Schmid confessed to dancing with the Devil, whom she described as acting like a tipsy youth. She stated that they were "each dancing round the other, pushing each other back and forth."[254]

The most frequently cited form of dance performed at the Sabbath was the ring dance. Some accounts of these dances were quite simple, such as that provided by Niclas Fiedler, who noted that his coven danced clumsily in a circle.[255] French woman Sybilla Morele gave the additional detail that when dancing in a circle, the Witches always moved to the left, or counterclockwise.[256] Still others provided more vivid descriptions, like that given by Jeanne Boisdeau. In her confession, she elaborated on how the Devil, in the form of a black goat, led a ring dance in which coven members held hands (the eldest member of the coven held the Devil's tail) with their backs turned to one another.[257] Witches dancing in a ring, facing outward and away from one another, is featured in numerous

---

252. Remy, *Demonolatry*, 60–61.

253. De Lancre, *On the Inconstancy of Witches*, 225.

254. Roper, *Witch Craze*, 109.

255. "The Confession of Niclas Fiedler at Trier, 1591," in *The Witchcraft Sourcebook*, 201.

256. Remy, *Demonolatry*, 61.

257. Pepper and Wilcock, *Magical and Mystical Sites: Europe and the British Isles*, 169–70.

Sabbath stories. Remy rationalized that the reason for this was either because Witches were afraid of being recognized by each other if they danced face to face or because of their love for doing things in a "ridiculous and unseemly manner."[258]

Music

Music was a common part of the Sabbath festivities, providing a backdrop of haunting tunes for the wild dances. Remy wrote that at the Sabbath "all is done to a marvellous medley and confusion of noises, and it is beyond the power of words to describe the uncouth, absurd and discordant sounds that are uttered there."[259] It was often the case that the music was played by select members of the coven or by the Devil himself. In regard to the former, while not a strict rule, it was often men who played music at the Sabbath meetings. When the Devil played, it was not always so melodious. For example, Scottish woman Isobel Cockie was accused of being at a Sabbath dance at which she grew displeased by the Devil's awful music. Believing that she could play better than him, she boldly snatched away his instrument and began to play herself—surprisingly without any reprimand for her brash behavior.[260] The music at the Sabbath was played using a wide range of instruments. In Switzerland, Jeanette Clerc confessed that they sang and danced to the music of a tambourine.[261] Meanwhile the accused Spanish Witches supposedly danced around illusionary fires to the music of timbrels, drums, and fiddles.[262] In England, Elizabeth Style mentioned that the Devil played a pipe or cittern while the coven danced about.[263] The Polish man Grzegorz reported that he played the dulcimer at the Sabbath meeting.[264]

---

258. Remy, *Demonolatry*, 61.

259. Remy, *Demonolatry*, 64–65.

260. The Spalding Club, *Miscellany of the Spalding Club*, 114–15.

261. Monter, *Witchcraft in France and Switzerland*, 57.

262. Frías, "An Account of the Persons at the Auto de Fe," in *The Salazar Documents*, 118.

263. Glanvill, *Saducismus Triumphatus*, 141.

264. Wyporska, *Witchcraft in Early Modern Poland 1500–1800*, 62.

In addition to musical instruments, at times the dancing would be accompanied by singing. For example, the Protestant preacher Bernhard Albrecht wrote that when the Witches danced, they would sing, "Har har, Devil, Devil, jump here, jump there, hop here, hop there, play here, play there," while lifting their hands and brooms high in order to demonstrate their fidelity to the Devil.[265] Helen Guthrie confessed that Andrew Watson sang old ballads and that Isobell Shyrie sang her song "Tinkletum Tankletum."[266] Maria Gleichmann admitted that in addition to the sound of drums, a big fiddle, and pipes at the Sabbath, she also heard "cheeky boy" songs, or songs that contained sexual references and insults toward neighbors.[267] Agnes Sampson confessed that at her meeting in the North Berwick churchyard, the Witches danced to a reel that went, "Commer goe ye before, commer goe ye. Gif ye will not goe before, commer let me."[268] And while not necessarily a song in the strictest sense of the word, the accused Witches of Mora, Sweden would vocalize by swearing and cursing while they performed their dances at Blåkulla.[269] Besides the coven members, the Devil would also sometimes perform songs at the Sabbath. Marie Lamont of Scotland confessed in 1662 that at a meeting, which took place at the home of Kattrein Scot, the Devil sang to the Witches while they danced around.[270] Additionally, in one unique case Anne Armstrong testified that after having been bewitched and ridden to the Sabbath, she was asked to sing for the Witches, which she shockingly agreed to do.[271]

---

265. Roper, *Witch Craze*, 113.

266. Kinloch, *Reliquiae Antiquae Scoticae*, 120.

267. Roper, *Witch Craze*, 109.

268. James Carmichael, "Newes from Scotland, declaring the damnable life and death of Doctor Fian a notable sorcerer […]" (London: [E. Allde?], c. 1542; Ann Arbor, MI: Text Creation Partnership, 2011).

269. Horneck, "An Account of What Happened in the Kingdom of Sweden in the Years 1669, and 1670," in Glanvill, *Saducismus Triumphatus*, 322.

270. Charles Kirkpatrick Sharpe, *A Historical Account of the Belief in Witchcraft in Scotland* (London: Hamilton, Adams & Co., 1884), 131.

271. Hole, *Witchcraft in England*, 124.

Sex at the Sabbath

While the Witches' Sabbath, at least in part, represented a diverse medley of pleasurable sins, it was acts of sexual congress that stood out as particularly licentious. During a time when sex was considered morally shameful, persecutors and writers on the subject of Witchcraft became highly fixated on the notion of the Witch as a sexually devious being. Their obsession with sex can be seen in trial transcripts and other texts, which border on pornographic in their descriptions. By interrogating accused Witches or writing about them, it seems that these men found a socially acceptable outlet for exploring their own repressed sexuality. Although there are sexual accounts of male Witches, by and large they are expressly focused on women. As such, there is a vividly clear theme of misogyny in these documents, which expose the deeply-rooted patriarchal beliefs regarding the nature of women. For example, the *Malleus Maleficarum* infamously states that "all witchcraft comes from carnal lust, which is in women insatiable."[272]

Stories of sexual activity at the Sabbath were normally concentrated specifically on copulation between Witches and the Devil. Accounts of such affairs are often quite confusing and full of contradicting details. For example, it was frequently intimated that sex with the Devil was physically uncomfortable or painful—typically because he was said to have a grotesquely large or otherwise deformed phallus. In some cases these liaisons even appear to have been coerced or overtly non-consensual. Yet, many accused Witches seemed to have had unexpected reactions to such ordeals, ranging from blasé to euphoric. For example, de Lancre noted several disturbing and graphic details regarding intercourse with the Devil while also sharing that accused Witches expressed pride and believed "the caresses of this filthy demon [the Devil] to be more worthy than those of the most just husband they could ever meet."[273] Again, it was almost exclusively women who were said to have sex with the Devil. When men

---

272. Kramer and Sprenger, *The Malleus Maleficarum*, 47.
273. De Lancre, *On the Inconstancy of Witches*, 233.

confessed to having had relations with the Devil, it was nearly always the case that the former appeared in the shape of a woman. Therefore, same-sex couplings were virtually nonexistent in trial confessions across Europe and in the early American colonies.

Whether sex with the Devil was meant to be pleasurable or not, there were thought to be two other motivating factors behind his desire to fornicate with Witches. First, it was claimed that by enticing Witches into sexual acts, the Devil could further corrupt their souls. When discussing sexual congress between humans and demons, de Lancre wrote that instead of partaking for pleasure, "they do it only in order to make man fall into the same precipice where they are, which is the disgrace of the Almighty."[274] He went on to mention how an accused Witch told him that "the Devil hardly ever had intercourse with virgins, because with them he could not commit adultery; thus he waits for them to be married."[275] Second, carnal relations were commonly believed to be one of the ways in which the initiatory pact between a Witch and the Devil was sealed. For example, Boguet expressed his belief that "the Devil uses them [Witches] so because he knows that women love carnal pleasures, and he means to bind them to his allegiance by such agreeable provocations."[276]

Sex at the Sabbath also included trysts between Witches. The unnamed Witch at Eichstätt confessed that after they had finished dancing, couples "paired off to commit lewdness on the side."[277] Jeanette d'Abadie confessed that at the Sabbath she saw men and women engage in "promiscuous activity."[278] The pairing of couples often fell back on the age-old stereotype of incestuous behavior that plagued earlier groups. As such, Boguet noted that "after the dancing the witches begin to couple with each other; and in this matter the son does not spare his mother, nor the brother his sister, nor the

---

274. De Lancre, *On the Inconstancy of Witches*, 232.

275. De Lancre, *On the Inconstancy of Witches*, 235.

276. Boguet, *An Examen of Witches*, 29.

277. "The Witch-Hunt at Eichstätt," in *The Witchcraft Sourcebook*, 224.

278. De Lancre, *On the Inconstancy of Witches*, 238.

father his daughter; but incest is commonly practised."[279] Furthermore, it was mentioned that the accused Witches of Spain "commit the vilest, obscenest, uncleanest acts without taking into consideration the degrees of kinship." It is also within the accounts of the Spanish Witch Trials that we find a rare reference to same-sex copulation, specifically regarding male Witches having had sex with both women and men.[280]

One of the major questions that arose in the mind of persecutors and writers was whether or not pregnancy could result from a human having sex with the Devil or some other demon. The general consensus was that, because of their non-corporeal bodies, these infernal spirits lacked the necessary components to impregnate a human woman. That being said, many texts cited the Dominican friar Thomas Aquinas, who explained how demons found a rather convoluted solution to this problem. According to Aquinas, a demon would first appear to a human man in the form of a woman in order to steal their semen. Said demon would then take that semen and, in the form of a man, inseminate a human woman. Thus, pregnancy could occur from such unholy unions, but the resulting child would not be a product of the demon itself.[281] Witches appeared to have been divided on the matter. For instance, Jeanette d'Abadie stated that "women never become pregnant from these copulations, whether they were with the master or with other witches."[282] Meanwhile, the accused Witches of Mora, Sweden, confessed that they would have sons and daughters with the Devil.[283]

The Sabbath in Art: Robert Burns's "Tam o' Shanter"

A more festive description of the activities at the Witches' Sabbath was included in Robert Burns's narrative poem "Tam o' Shanter." Written in

---

279. Boguet, *An Examen of Witches*, 57.

280. Frías, "An Account of the Persons at the Auto de Fe," in *The Salazar Documents*, 124.

281. Boguet, *An Examen of Witches*, 36.

282. De Lancre, *On the Inconstancy of Witches*, 238.

283. Horneck, "An Account of What Happened in the Kingdom of Sweden in the Years 1669, and 1670," in Glanvill, *Saducismus Triumphatus*, 322–23.

1790 and published the following year, the poem tells the story of Tam, a blundering farmer who often gets drunk at a local public house.

One stormy night, Tam is riding home upon his trusted horse Maggie when he spies a glowing light coming from the nearby church:

> *When, glimmering thro' the groaning trees,*
> *Kirk-Alloway seem'd in a bleeze:*
> *Thro' ilka bore the beams were glancing,*
> *And loud resounded mirth and dancing.*

Motivated by a sense of curiosity and alcohol-induced bravery, Tam ventures closer to the church in order to find the source of the light. Peering through a window into the church, Tam is astonished to witness a gathering of Witches dancing with the Devil:

> *Warlocks and witches in a dance;*
> *Nae cotillon, brent new frae France,*
> *But hornpipes, jigs, strathspeys, and reels*
> *Put life and mettle in their heels.*
> *A winnock bunker in the east,*
> *There sat Auld Nick in shape o' beast;*
> *A towzie tyke, black, grim, and large,*
> *To gie them music was his charge;*
> *He screw'd the pipes and gart them skirl,*
> *Till roof and rafters a' did dirl.*

The poem goes on to describe the way in which the church has been decorated with several macabre items. Around the room, coffins stand open with each corpse holding aloft a lit candle that helps illuminate the devilish convocation. Upon the holy altar lies many dark objects, including the bones of a murderer, bloodstained tomahawks, a garter that had strangled a baby, and a knife used by a son to slit his own father's throat. Tam continues to watch the dance, entranced by the movements of the women—particularly that of a beautiful Witch dressed in a short skirt.

Lost in his own lust, Tam foolishly lets out a cry that immediately alerts the Witches to his intrusion at their Sabbath:

> And [Tam] roars out, "Weel done, Cutty-sark!"
> And in an instant all was dark:
> And scarcely had he Maggie rallied.
> When out the hellish legion sallied.

A dramatic chase ensues with Tam, riding upon Maggie, being pursued by the furious horde of Witches. Luckily, Tam spots a running stream, which he knows the Witches cannot cross, and steers Maggie in its direction. At the climax of the poem, Tam and Maggie make it over the bridge, just narrowly escaping the clutches of the angry Witches—although it is noted that one of the Witches snatches off poor Maggie's tail, leaving nothing but a stump.[284]

While "Tam o' Shanter" explores themes regarding the fleeting nature of life's pleasures, as well as the consequences of one's actions, it also contains interesting pieces of Witch folklore still popular during Burns's lifetime. In fact, shortly before the poem was written, Burns had penned a letter to his friend Francis Grose in which he provided three different stories regarding Witches and the Alloway church. Two of these stories he regarded as being authentic accounts of Witches, one of which was the basis for what would later become "Tam o' Shanter."[285] Whether or not Alloway church was ever used as a meeting place for Witches, Burns's poem paints a vivid picture of the Sabbath as it was believed to have taken place. For instance, it was common within Scottish folklore for Sabbath meetings to occur within local churches. Additionally, Scottish accounts of the Sabbath were usually centered around rowdy music and dancing. "Tam o' Shanter" does an excellent job at conveying, through both its imagery and meter, the sort of ecstatic freedom Witches felt at the Sabbath.

---

284. Robert Burns, "Tam o' Shanter," Poetry Foundation, accessed February 5, 2021, https://www.poetryfoundation.org/poems/43815/tam-o-shanter.

285. "Tam o' Shanter," Burns Country, accessed February 5, 2021, http://www.robertburns .org/encyclopedia/TamOShanter.23.shtml.

Despite the grisly decor all around them, the Witches in Burns's poem find much merriment in their rambunctious capering, perhaps itself a representation of finding pleasure and power in (or in spite of) the darkness.

Chapter 8
DANCING THE
DEVIL'S GROUND

At this point, we've uncovered the historical development of the Witches' Sabbath, from early accusations lodged against Christians to supposed poisonous plots hatched by those suffering from leprosy. We've explored the ways in which beliefs regarding heresy blended with folkloric stories about various Witch-like spirits. We've examined the Sabbath's re-emergence in the practice of modern Witchcraft and the different ways it took hold, from the Witch-Cult Hypothesis to the work of those like Andrew Chumbley. We dove into the architecture of the Otherworld and developed the skills and gathered the tools necessary to make our own journey to the Witches' Sabbath. We've met the spirits who compose the Sabbath's company and discovered the ways in which we can work with them. Finally, we've learned of the acts of both business and pleasure that account for the Sabbath's activities, from rituals of initiation and malefica to frenetic ring dances and sumptuous feasts. And now here you are, on the precipice, approaching the hedge.

In this chapter we will take all of our loose threads and unite them once more, weaving that original tapestry back together. But it will not be unchanged, as you are about to become a part of the very narrative it depicts. And so, using the collective knowledge gained from the previous chapters, we will work to formulate a ritualized plan for your visit to the legendary Witches' Sabbath. In this final chapter you will find some of my final advice on spirit flight, additional tools to help you on your journey into the Otherworld, and rituals for traveling to the Sabbath ground. Additionally, you will find helpful prompts for conjuring forth a specific Sabbath experience as well as a ritual enactment of the Sabbath for coven work in the physical realm.

Some Final Advice

One of the biggest pieces of advice I can give to someone who is new to Otherworldly travel and visiting the Witches' Sabbath is to not put pressure on yourself or your experience. I have found over the years that the process of spirit flight is often thought of or described in ways that are overly exaggerated—whether that is intentional or not. Many people go into it with high expectations, typically that their spirit will become completely severed from their physical body and that they will have extremely vivid experiences characterized by intense sights and sounds. However, you will quickly come to realize that this just isn't the case. Even while you're in the Otherworld, you will retain some cognizance of your physical body—you may even hear sounds from the physical world. And that's okay! Additionally, sensory perceptions of the Otherworld will vary. You might have a difficult time seeing the Otherworld or the Sabbath clearly but you are able to hear or feel it. Again, this is okay! It is often the case that when we put pressure on ourselves or on our experiences, the results end up being less than satisfactory. Just keep trying. The more you practice, the stronger and sharper your skills will become.

The second piece of advice I have is to limit the frequency of Otherworldly journeys and visits to the Sabbath. While it may be tempting to spend a great deal of time engaging in spirit flight, the more time we spend in the Otherworld, the more we become susceptible to a handful of negative symptoms. For example, it is not uncommon for someone in that situation to begin feeling detached from the reality of the mundane world as well as from their physical body. Other times one may become depressed, apathetic, or withdrawn. Therefore, I recommend limiting the frequency of Otherworldly journeys and visits to the Sabbath, especially in the beginning, to two times a month. I like to plan these occasions around the full and new moon or some other auspicious day, such as Halloween or Walpurgisnacht.

Finally, I highly encourage you to write down your experiences when you return from the Sabbath. In my own experience, I've noticed that the finer details of Otherworldly journeys tend to fade quickly once I've come back to the physical world. Therefore, I highly recommend that you keep a journal nearby and that you write down your experiences before they slip away. If you are artistically inclined, you could even create a drawing or painting of the Sabbath from which you have just returned. You will then be able to revisit these documentations later for further reflection if need be. Additionally, over time you may start to recognize patterns within your recorded experiences—providing further knowledge about yourself, the spirits with whom you work, and Craft itself.

Additional Sabbath Tools

In addition to the tools of mind and body discussed in chapter 4, there are also physical tools that can be useful when venturing into the Otherworld and traveling to the Witches' Sabbath. These tools are ones that are meant to be crafted by your own hand, infused with your magic and a part of your very spirit. Each tool serves a unique purpose, but they all also house their own innate spirit and magic. By creating these tools yourself, you not only help awaken the indwelling spirit to their purpose but also form an inherently deep relationship with them as well. Armed with these tools, you will be better equipped to lift your spirit from your physical body, find your way into the Otherworld, and safely navigate yourself toward the Witches' Sabbath. These tools include a broomstick and an anchoring talisman.

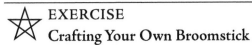 EXERCISE
Crafting Your Own Broomstick

Like the Witches' of folklore, your own spirit flight may be helped along with the use of some physical implement to ride upon. For this specific purpose, the following exercise can be used in order to create a broomstick that can be used when journeying to the Sabbath.

Necessary Items
Sturdy branch approximately 60 inches in length

Sharp knife

Sandpaper

Wood burner (optional)

Wood stain

Linseed oil

Rags

Paints and brushes (optional)

Bundle of dried straw or grass

Good length of hemp or jute cord

Broomstick Handle
Begin by going out to some wild, natural place where you will be able to find a sturdy branch that will become the handle for your broomstick. Keep in mind that the average length for a broom handle is approximately 60 inches, but feel free to make adjustments to accommodate your own unique height. You will also want to consider the different types of wood and their inherent virtues: for example, ash wood has long been associated with the Otherworld and broom crafting.

If you intend to cut a live branch, make sure to ask the indwelling spirit of that tree for permission first. Allow your mind to become open and aware of the spirit's voice and whether its message is affirmative or negative. If the spirit does not wish for you to take its branch, you will have to move on. If the spirit agrees, cut the branch as cleanly as possible using a sharpened saw.

Make sure to leave an offering of honey or water at the base of the tree. It is also possible to find a branch that has naturally fallen. In this case, it is still important to leave an offering for the spirits of the land. If using a freshly cut branch, or if the wood is not completely dry, place it aside for some time and allow it to dry out completely before proceeding to the next step. Make sure to store the branch horizontally as it dries in order to avoid bowing.

Next, carefully strip away any bark using a sharp knife. Then, smooth down the handle with different textured sandpaper. At this point, you can use a woodburning tool to inscribe the handle with various magical symbols that have particular meaning to you. For example, you might include a pentagram, runes, or astrological symbols. Finally, you can stain your broom handle and finish it off with a protective coating of linseed oil, using rags for the application of both. If you don't have a woodburning tool or don't feel comfortable using one, you can also use paint to apply your symbols to the broom handle after the staining process but before coating it with oil.

Broomstick Brush

For your broomstick's brush you have a few different options. First, you can go out into the wild and collect a bunch of dried grass, wispy twigs, or straw. If you decide to harvest the brush yourself, make sure to first ask permission from the indwelling spirit of whichever material you plan on using. Allow your mind to become open and aware of the spirit's voice and whether its message is affirmative or negative. If the spirit does not wish for you to use its material, you will have to move on. If the spirit agrees, only harvest as much as you will realistically need and leave an offering of thanks nearby. Second, you can purchase a cheap broomcorn broomstick and repurpose its brush by cutting it loose from the handle. Third, you can purchase loose broomcorn or other brush for your broomstick from online sources.

Assembling Your Broomstick

Once you are ready to assemble your broomstick, gather the handle, brush, and length of cord. Lay the brush on a flat surface, spreading it out evenly and place the handle in the middle of it. Then, gather up the brush around the handle, adjusting it so that it is evenly dispersed. Using the length of cord, wrap it tightly around the brush once—tying an initial knot and making sure to leave some excess cord to use for the final knot at the end. Continue wrapping the cord around the brush, periodically pulling tightly. Keep wrapping until the brush feels securely fastened to the broom handle. Finally, using the excess cord, tie three knots for luck.

Hallowing Your Broomstick

To *hallow*, or bless, your new broomstick with magical virtue, begin by lighting some strong, aromatic incense (I recommend using the Hedge Witch Incense on page 95). Then, fanning the smoke along the length of the broomstick, recite the following incantation:

> *Broomstick made from branch and straw,*
> *To the Sabbath, my spirit you'll draw,*
> *From my home and across the sky,*
> *A sturdy stead to help me fly*
> *And to bring me home when all is done*
> *Or with the rising of the morning sun.*

 EXERCISE
Creating an Anchoring Talisman

While the spirit does leave the physical body in order to travel into the Otherworld, there remains an important tether between the two. To secure this connection, you can create a talisman for the purposes of anchoring your spirit to your body.

Necessary Items
Medium-size flat stone
Paint (black, white, red, blue, and green)
Fine-tipped paintbrush

To begin, go out into some wild, natural place where you can find a medium-size flat stone. Ideally, this stone should be the size of your open palm and have some weight to it. When you find a suitable stone, make sure to ask its indwelling spirit if it wishes to work with you. If the answer is no, gently replace the stone where you found it and continue your search. Once you have found your stone, leave an offering of honey or water on the ground nearby. Take the stone home and wash it in cool water to rinse away any dirt or dust. Allow it to dry in a warm, sunny spot before moving on to the next step.

Using your paint and brush, copy the following sigil onto the surface of your stone. This sigil depicts the six roads of the compass round: north/air, east/fire, south/earth, west/water, Upperworld/white crescent, and Underworld/black crescent. Arrows along each road, pointing toward the center of the compass, symbolize the anchoring of your spirit to your body as it rests in the center, or in the Midworld. Take your time and focus on the magical virtues of the stone melding with your own intentions of anchoring your spirit while engaging in Otherworldly travel. When you're finished, return the stone to a warm, sunny spot and let the paint dry thoroughly.

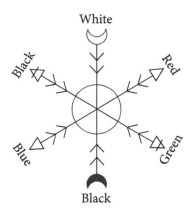

To hallow your new talisman, pass it through some cleansing, aromatic smoke. Whisper to the stone your intentions and what you desire from its spirit. Then, recite the following spell thrice to finalize the ritual:

By painted symbol upon this stone,
Anchor my spirit to flesh and to bone.
Allow my soul to separate and lift
But not to go too far adrift.

 ### EXERCISE
A Simple Sabbath Ritual

The following ritual is basic in nature and serves as a good starting point for anyone who is new to traveling into the Otherworld or attending the Witches' Sabbath. Additionally, this ritual can be performed anytime, although the night of a full or new moon is particularly auspicious, and can be done indoors or outdoors.

Optional Items

Blanket and pillow
Candles
Incense
Flying ointment, tea, or tincture
Broomstick
Pre-recorded music
Protective charm bag and/or anchoring stone

Preparation of Space

Begin by preparing your physical space. The number one thing that you will want to do is eliminate as many distractions as possible. If you live with other people, explain to them that you need some time alone and that you are not to be disturbed. If you have pets, contain them in an appropriate manner or have someone else watch over them. You will want to lie down during your Otherworldly travel, whether that be on a bed or on the floor. If doing the latter, you might wish you spread out a blanket and throw down a pillow or two to support your head. You want your body to be as comfortable as possible in order to minimize somatic distractions.

If you plan on having pre-recorded music playing, now is the time to set that up and to make sure it will run smoothly. Additionally, light any incense or candles—being mindful of fire safety.

Preparation of Body

Once your space is ready, you'll want to take some time to prepare your body. If you are making use of a flying ointment, tea, or tincture, now is the time to do so—remember that it will take approximately 30 minutes to take effect. Additionally, you will want to adorn yourself with any protective amulets. Then, once you are lying down, place your broomstick vertically on the ground next to you or horizontally with the handle underneath your knees. You will also want to have your anchoring talisman either in one of your hands or flat on your chest or stomach. Finally, if you notice your body feeling tense, make use of the progressive muscle relaxation exercise found on page 83.

Into the Otherworld

Now that your space and physical body have been prepared, it's time to travel into the Otherworld. Begin by closing your eyes and starting the box breathing technique. Take in a nice breath, hold for a moment, exhale smoothly, hold once more, and then start the cycle over. Repeat this cycle 11 more times, for a total of 12 repetitions, counting down in your mind as you go. With each breath, feel your spirit lifting up out of your physical body, pulling away gently. You might simultaneously feel your physical body sinking, a sensation of being both heavy and numb. Next, take yourself even deeper into your trance state by repeating the above process but with 13 cycles this time, again counting down as you go along. When you reach number 6, picture in your mind's eye that you are standing before a hedgerow. Just beyond this boundary is a swirling gray fog that obscures your vision. As you get closer to number 1, take a running leap and jump over the hedgerow. Feel your feet land firmly upon the ground in the Otherworld as you reach the end of the countdown.

To the Witches' Sabbath

As the fog lifts, you will find yourself standing in front of the axis mundi. Allow the axis to appear to you as it will—likely in the same form it took during the exercise in chapter 4.

For the purpose of attending the Witches' Sabbath, you will be remaining in the hidden landscape of the Midworld. Look down to find your broomstick in hand. Mount the broom and speak the words "Thout, tout a tout, tout, throughout and about." With that you will be swiftly carried off to the Sabbath ground. The journey will vary in length, sometimes seeming quite long and other times instantaneous. The location of the Sabbath will differ as well and may take on the appearance of a place from the mundane world or somewhere that exists only in the Otherworld. Wherever you end up, allow your spirit to land softly on the ground.

The Sabbath

As with many of the other aspects of this ritual, the Sabbath itself will fluctuate in its appearance to you. That being said, there will likely be a large bonfire blazing in the center of a circle composed of Witches and various spirits. Additionally, at the head of the assembly might be the Devil and Sabbath Queen sitting atop ornately crafted thrones. What unfolds at the Sabbath will likely follow the folklore in regard to acts of business and pleasure. You might learn new spells or perform certain rituals. You might dance, feast, or engage in sexual activity if so desired. The possibilities are truly endless. It's best to allow the experience to flow organically and to allow yourself to go along for the ride. This means letting go of a certain amount of control, but rest assured that you can leave at any point if you begin to feel overwhelmed or uncomfortable (follow the next steps).

Coming Home

At whatever point you desire to return from the Sabbath, look down to find your broomstick in hand. Mount your broom and speak the words "Rentum Tormentum." With that, you will be carried off by the wind. You will travel across the sky, going back the way you came, all the way to the axis mundi. Once you have returned to the axis, begin to count upward from 1 to 13. When you reach number 6, turn to see the same hedge you initially crossed over when entering the Otherworld. Again, take a running leap and jump over the hedgerow. Feel your feet land firmly upon the ground in the mundane world. When you've got your bearings, count upward once more, this time from 1 to 12. As you progress through your countdown, feel yourself coming back into full awareness. Wiggle your fingers and your toes, then your arms and legs. When you feel ready, slowly open your eyes and feel yourself return to a state of full consciousness.

 EXERCISE
A Complex Sabbath Ritual

The following ritual is slightly more complex than the previous one as it utilizes both the ritual of laying a compass round and treading the mill in order to help aid the journey into the Otherworld and to the Witches' Sabbath. As before, this ritual can be performed anytime and can be done indoors or outdoors, although I personally find that this one works particularly well when done outside.

Necessary Items
Object to act as a focal point (perhaps a lantern or a stang)
Hedge Witch Incense (see page 95)
White or black pillar candle
Stone
Small bowl of water

Optional Items
Blanket and pillow
Broomstick
Protective charm bag and/or anchoring talisman
Pre-recorded music
Flying ointment, tea, or tincture

Preparation of Space

For this ritual, you will need a lot more space than the previous one in order to accommodate both laying a compass round and treading the mill. Additionally, unlike the previous version of this ritual, you will need to be able to lie on the ground. You can prepare the space by spreading out a blanket and a pillow if you so desire. If you plan on using a broomstick, protective charm bag, or anchoring talisman, you can place these by your blanket or designated resting area. As before, do your best to eliminate as many distractions as you can. If you live with other people, explain to them that you need some time alone and that you are not to be disturbed. If you have pets, contain them in an appropriate manner or have someone else watch over them. If you plan on having pre-recorded music playing, now is the time to set that up and to make sure it will run smoothly.

Preparation of Body

Once your space is ready, you'll want to take some time to prepare your body. If you are making use of a flying ointment, tea, or tincture, now is the time to do so—remember that it will take approximately 30 minutes to take effect. Additionally, you will want to adorn yourself with any protective amulets.

Laying the Compass Round

Begin by placing your focal object in the center of your space. Then, starting in the north, stand with your feet firmly planted on the ground. In your hand, hold the burning incense, fan your fingers through the smoke, and smell its rich scent. Close your eyes and take in a deep breath. Feel yourself reaching out to the spirits of the northern road. When you feel connected, say aloud,

> *I call to the spirits of the north, primal powers of air and wind. I kindly ask that you open the roadways into your realm. Come, join my compass round!*

Move to the east, standing with your feet firmly planted on the ground. In your hand, hold the flickering candle, pass a finger quickly near the flame, and feel its heat. Close your eyes and take in a deep breath. Feel yourself reaching out to the spirits of the eastern road. When you feel connected, say aloud,

> *I call to the spirits of the east, primal powers of fire and flame. I kindly ask that you open the roadways into your realm. Come, join my compass round!*

Move to the south, standing with your feet firmly planted on the ground. In your hand, hold the stone, run your fingers over its surface, and feel its solid mass. Close your eyes and take in a deep breath. Feel yourself reaching out to the spirits of the southern road. When you feel connected, say aloud,

> *I call to the spirits of the south, primal powers of earth and stone. I kindly ask that you open the roadways into your realm. Come, join my compass round!*

Move to the west, standing with your feet firmly planted on the ground. In your hand, hold the bowl of water, dip your finger in, and feel the coolness. Close your eyes and take in a deep breath. Feel yourself reaching out to the spirits of the western road. When you feel connected, say aloud,

> *I call to the spirits of the west, primal powers of water and sea. I kindly ask that you open the roadways into your realm. Come, join my compass round!*

Move to the center of the circle, standing with your feet firmly planted on the ground. Raise your arms above your head, spreading your fingers and reaching as high as you can. Close your eyes and take in a deep breath. Feel yourself reaching out to the spirits of the upper road. When you feel connected, say aloud,

I call to the spirits of above, primal powers of the Upperworld. I kindly ask that you open the roadways into your realm. Come, join my compass round!

Remaining in the center of the circle, standing with your feet firmly planted on the ground. Lower your arms toward the ground, spreading your fingers and reaching as low as you can. Close your eyes and take in a deep breath. Feel yourself reaching out to the spirits of the lower road. When you feel connected, say aloud,

I call to the spirits of below, primal powers of the Underworld. I kindly ask that you open the roadways into your realm. Come, join my compass round!

Treading the Mill

To start, decide whether you are going to be pacing clockwise or counterclockwise. If you choose to pace clockwise, stand with your right shoulder parallel to the central focal point. Keeping your body facing forward, extending your right arm outward, pointing your index finger at the central focal point. Turn your head to the side, cocking it back slightly so that your chin rests on your shoulder. Gaze down your arm and fix your sight on the central focal point. Then, begin to slowly walk forward, making sure to maintain eye contact with the central focal point. If choosing the counterclockwise, simply do the opposite, using the left side of your body. As you tread, you may wish to use the lame step. If that's the case, as you tread, allow your right (if pacing clockwise) or left foot (if pacing counterclockwise) to drag on the ground behind you.

Continue pacing, allowing the steady, monotonous motion to pull you into a deeper state of consciousness. Sense your mind becoming quiet and your eyesight starting to soften. As you tread, be mindful of your breathing, keeping it smooth and rhythmic. After a while, you may notice that you start to gain speed in your circling. If this feels comfortable for you, continue to gather momentum. Otherwise, simply slow your movements. Eventually, you will reach a point when the trance has taken hold and your spirit feels lifted. When this happens, stop in your tracks and quickly lie down upon your blanket or intended resting spot. Allow the force of the trance to carry your spirit up from your physical body and over the hedge into the Otherworld. You may experience this as a propulsion or other fast-paced flying sensation. Eventually, you'll feel your feet land firmly upon the ground in the Otherworld.

To the Witches' Sabbath

As in the previous version of this ritual, find yourself standing in front of the axis mundi. Look down to find your broomstick in hand. Mount the broom and speak the words "Thout, tout a tout, tout, throughout and about." With that you will be swiftly carried off to the Sabbath's location. Again, the journey will vary in length, sometimes seeming quite long and other times instantaneous. The location of the Sabbath will differ as well and may take on the appearance of a place from the mundane world or somewhere that exists only in the Otherworld. Wherever you end up, allow your spirit to land softly on the ground.

The Sabbath

As before, how the Sabbath appears to you and what takes place there will fluctuate. Give yourself over to the experience and remember that you can return whenever you wish.

Coming Home

At whatever point you desire to return from the Sabbath, look down to find your broomstick in hand. Mount your broom and speak the words "Rentum Tormentum." With that, you will be carried off by the wind. You will travel across the sky, going back the way you came, all the way to the axis mundi. Once you have returned to the axis mundi, utilize the same method for returning to the physical world as in the previous exercise— by counting upward from 1 to 13. When you reach number 6, turn to see the same hedge you initially crossed over when entering the Otherworld. Again, take a running leap and jump over the hedgerow. Feel your feet land firmly upon the ground in the mundane world. When you've got your bearings, count upward once more, this time from 1 to 12. As you progress through your countdown, feel yourself coming back into full awareness. Wiggle your fingers and your toes, then your arms and legs. When you feel ready, slowly open your eyes and feel yourself return to a state of full consciousness.

Sabbath Prompts

While it's true that the Sabbath typically proceeds of its own accord, we do have some amount of power to influence what occurs therein. Specifically, we can sway the intention or theme of the Sabbath before we even arrive. In order to do this, all you need to do is spend some time reflecting on the reason you will be attending the Sabbath, what you're hoping to accomplish or participate in while there, and what the overall setting will look like— including location, decorations, costuming, and ritual or spell implements. In doing so, you are effectively exerting your will into the Otherworld before traveling there, shaping the Sabbath to meet your needs. If you need help coming up with ideas for Sabbath themes, consider the following list. Please note that this list is composed of my own associations pulled from folklore. You will want to use imagery that speaks to your own imagination.

Honoring

In a firelit cavern, the spirits who are being honored sit upon special thrones ornately carved from dark wood. The Sabbath ground is infused with a sense of deep reverence. Those in attendance each carry an offering, which they take turns leaving at the feet of the spirits being honored. As you approach these spirits, you have the chance to speak words of honor and gratitude.

Initiation

A radiant full moon shines down from the dark night sky, illuminating the forest around you. Those in attendance wear black cloaks with masks disguising their faces. Before you is a stone altar, lit by various candles.

Upon the altar sits a tattered, ancient-looking black book. Wind stirs and howls through the trees as you prepare to add your name to those already scrawled across the yellowed pages.

Lunar

Standing in the middle of an expansive meadow, you are surrounded by other Witches. The air crackles with magical energy. Depending on the phase, there may be a brilliant full moon in the sky or nothing but inky black darkness. The altar resting in the center of the circle might be adorned with silver candles or perhaps it houses a large, dark mirror. Those in attendance could be bathed in moonlight or they could be flitting shadows moving across the dimly lit Sabbath ground. Together, you might pull the full moon's blessings or work darker, more introspective forms of magic on the new moon.

Seasonal

Depending on the season, you may find the Sabbath looks a number of different ways—as a cemetery in late autumn or perhaps an old stone circle at the height of spring. The ritual might be illuminated by twinkling lights strung up in snow-covered pines or by an enormous summer bonfire. Activities too will vary by season, such as invoking the dead in the last days of autumn or dancing with the Fair Folk to celebrate the arrival of spring. Riding upon the frosty night air alongside the Wild Hunt in the winter or working spells for blessings and purification at the height of summer.

Spellwork

On a particularly auspicious night, you find yourself on the peak of a desolate mountain high above the valley below. Depending upon the work at hand, you find the altar adorned accordingly. Spread upon its surface are all the tools you will need to cast your spell. You are joined by a coven of other Witches, dressed in cloaks whose color corresponds with your magical intentions. From the darker recesses of the Sabbath ground, the spirits approach, ready and willing to lend their powers to your spellwork.

✬ EXERCISE
Physical Sabbath Ritual for Coven Use

The following ritual is intended for the use of a coven seeking to enact the Witches' Sabbath in the physical, mundane world. The ritual is suitable for any size coven, although it may become more difficult to orchestrate with more than thirteen members. Additionally, the ritual can be performed indoors, but ideally it should take place outside in a secret, natural setting such as a forest or on a hilltop—or in your own backyard if you are lucky enough to have one. Whatever the chosen location, there will need to be enough space to accommodate your coven.

Furthermore, the ritual is to be led by two members who will take on the roles of Devil and Sabbath Queen. If needed or desired, one member can act as a solo leader, in which case the ritual structure will need to be modified. The Sabbath Queen should be dressed in a gown of white, gray, or green with a crown or some sort of headdress. The Devil should be clothed entirely in black with a mask or face covering as well as a brimmed hat or hood.

Finally, this ritual includes aspects of both business and pleasure but can be adjusted to include one or the other as you see fit. In fact, the ritual provided is meant to be a template you can tailor to your own Sabbath enactment. As such, feel free to rework the structure as well as to use your own words in place of those given. More often than not, this ritual will organically unfold into a completely unique experience each time it is performed.

Necessary Items

Cauldron (big enough to contain a small fire; if working indoors,
    use a large pillar candle)
4 lanterns
Loaf of bread
Bottle of wine or juice
Musical instruments (such as a drum, flute, or tambourine)
Incense

Candle

Stone

Bowl of water

Chalice or drinking cup (each coven member should bring their own)

Preparation of Space

Before the ritual begins, whichever coven members will be playing the role of Sabbath leaders must go to the designated spot and prepare the space. The rest of the coven will need to be somewhere else, far enough away so that they cannot see the preparation but close enough to hear a signal telling them when to approach. Place the cauldron in the center of the space, with the fire or candle burning within. Additionally, position a lantern at each of the four directions—make sure that there will be enough space for your coven to move about within the perimeter of these lanterns. The bread, wine, and musical instruments can be set down near the northern lantern. Following the same instructions as given in chapter 4, the leaders should now lay a compass round, finishing with the following words:

> *By the laying of this compass round,*
> *We conjure forth the Sabbath ground.*

When the ritual area has been fully prepared, the leaders can signal for the rest of the coven to approach by sounding a musical instrument. As the coven members approach, they should each make a low bow before entering the compass round. Once inside, they should gather around the burning cauldron, forming a circle. The leaders should be standing in the north. When everyone has entered the ritual space, the Devil announces,

> *Merry meet, Witches. Tonight we gather, in honor of our folkloric ancestors, to enact the Sabbath rite. We come together in this place, to practice our sorcerous art and to give ourselves over to the ecstasies of the eldritch world beyond.*

It is at this point that any spellwork or spirit communion may take place. How the coven members are directed from this point forward will be dependent upon the specific workings at hand. When the work is done, coven members should be directed to once again assemble around the burning cauldron with the leaders positioned in the north. When everyone is in place, the Devil announces,

> *By our words and by our deeds, the Witching work is now complete.*
> *And so, the time has come for us to partake in the bread and the wine*
> *of the Sabbath rite.*

The Devil now holds the bread aloft and proclaims,

> *By my name, this bread be hallowed.*

The Sabbath Queen follows suit, holding the bottle of wine aloft and proclaiming,

> *By my name, this wine be hallowed.*

The Devil then goes around distributing a small piece of bread to each coven member. Meanwhile, the Sabbath Queen pours a bit of wine into each of the coven member's drinking cups.

When every Witch has both bread and wine, the Sabbath Queen speaks,

> *Eat and drink, both in our names,*
> *The Man in Black and Sabbath Dame.*
> *Taste these gifts of wine and bread,*
> *With little sadness and no dread.*

The coven members can now eat their bread and drink their wine. While waiting for everyone to finish, coven members who brought instruments should begin to play. Once the majority of the coven members have finished, the Devil speaks:

> *Go forth, make merry, in both of our names,*
> *And so begin the Sabbath games!*

The rest of the Sabbath may be spent dancing, singing, and making merry. If the numbers allow it, I recommend performing a traditional ring dance—with each coven member facing outward, arms linked, and the circle spinning to the left.

When, at last, the time comes for the ritual to end, the music stops and the Devil speaks,

The time has come for the Sabbath's end,
Back to your homes we do thee send,
Now leave this place, go on depart,
A Boy! Merry meet, merry part! [286]

Each member may now exit the compass round, making a low bow as they do. From there, they should each return the way they originally came. Meanwhile, the leaders will bid farewell to the directional spirits called upon when laying the compass round. They will then clean up the ritual space and safely put out the fire.

---

286. This last line comes directly from the confession of Elizabeth Style. See Glanvill, *Saducismus Triumphatus*, 141.

CONCLUSION

It is my hope that whether you planned on traveling to the Sabbath yourself or you were merely a curious researcher, this book has proved to be useful in your endeavors. Witchcraft is rooted in myth and its modern practice is born from a legacy of ever-evolving, ever-shifting folklore. Whether we are aware of it or not, the threads of our modern Craft are spun forth from the diverse tales of magic and Witchery that have been told around the world for hundreds of years. And if there has been one particular piece of lore that has been most central to the expansion of Witchcraft mythology, and thus our own practices today, it is that of the Witches' Sabbath. It is from the stories given about such nocturnal meetings that we have learned about topics like spirit fight, flying ointment, auspicious days and locations, implements of flight, covens and their structure, initiation rituals, spirit work, magical spells and rituals, and so much more. Therefore, the Sabbath can be viewed as more than just a gathering of Witches and spirits, but also as a metaphoric cauldron of convalescing beliefs and practices.

Both Austin Osman Spare and Kenneth Grant espoused the power of atavistic resurgence, and I too believe that there is magic to be found in following a trail backward in time, in search of connection to something vast and primal. The goal of this book was to do just that, to wander along a folkloric path leading into the hidden depths of history wherein the Witches' Sabbath emerged. Spare and Grant believed that in seeking out the source that lay at the end of such atavistic roadways, one could merge with a current of power invaluable to Witches, magicians, and mystics alike. While there are likely many different atavistic sources, I believe that for practitioners of Witchcraft, particularly those of a Traditional persuasion, the Otherworldly Sabbath is one of special importance. For it is here we find the many pieces of our folkloric heritage as practitioners of the Craft coming together across space and time—forming a nexus of primal energy that can be tapped into as a means of magical and spiritual empowerment. And as part of the legacy of our Craft, we possess the same power as our folkloric forebears to send our spirits out into the night, flying off to some mystical locale where the Sabbath unfolds before our very eyes. So fly forth, Witches!

ACCUSED WITCHES

The following list contains the names of the accused Witches mentioned throughout this book. The names of the accused Witches are organized by country and include the date (if known) that they were brought to trial.

Countries

Early American Colonies

Abigail Hobbes, 1692

Ann Foster, 1692

George Burroughs, 1692

Martha Carrier, 1692

Mary Osgood, 1692

Mary Toothaker, 1692

Mary Warren, 1692

Rebecca Greensmith, 1663

William Baker Sr., 1692

England

Alice Duke

Anne Armstrong, 1673

Anne Dryden, 1673

Anne Forster, 1673

Elizabeth Style, 1664

Luce Thompson, 1673

Margaret Johnson, 1633

Mary Green, 1665

France

Antoine Tornier

Barbelina Rayel, 1587

Catharine de Nagiulle

Clauda Jamguillaume

Clauda Vuillat

Claudette Delat, 1608

Claudon Bregeat, 1612

Didier Pierrat, 1597

Dominique Isabelle, 1583

Guillaume Edelin, 1453

Isaac de Queyran, 1609

Jacquema Paget

Jeanette d'Abadie, 1609

Jeanne Boisdeau, 1594

La Grande Lucye, 1608

Margueritte le Charpentier, 1620

Marie Balcoin

Marie d'Aspilcoutte

Sybilla Morele, 1586

Ysabeau Richard, 1615

Germany

Barbara Schluchter, 1617

Johannes Junius, 1628

Maria Gleichmann, 1617

Niclas Fiedler, 1591

Waldburga Schmid, 1626

Walpurga Hausmännin, 1587

Unnamed Woman from Eichstätt, 1637

Unnamed Woman from Bern, 1630

Guernsey

Collette Du Mont, 1617

Isabel Becquet, 1617

Marie Becquet, 1617

Italy

Margherita of San Roco, 1571

Matteuccia Francisci, 1428

Pierina de Bripio, 1390

Sibillia de Fraguliati, 1384

Unnamed Woman, 1588

Vicencia la Rosa, 1630

Scotland

Agnes Cairnes, 1659

Agnes Sampson, 1590

Alexander Elder, 1662

Alison Pearson, 1588

Andrew Watson, 1661

Andro Man, 1598

Bessie Dunlop, 1576

Bessie Weir, 1677

Elspet Alexander, 1661

Helen Guthrie, 1663

Hellen Alexander, 1661

Isobel Cockie, 1597

Isobel Gowdie, 1662

Isobell Shyrie, 1661

Issobell Dorward

Issobell Smyth, 1661

James Lindsay, 1697

Janet Breadheid, 1662

Jean Mairten, 1662

John Taylor, 1662

Johne Young, 1662

Jonet Howat, 1661

Kattrein Scott, 1662

Mairie Rynd, 1661

Margaret Brodie, 1662

Margaret Talzeor, 1658

Marie Lamont, 1662

Marion Grant, 1597

Sweden

Unnamed men, women, and children from Mora, 1669

Switzerland

Anthonia Preudhon, 1583

Gonin Depertyt, 1606

Jeanette Clerc, 1539

Madeleine Merlou, 1583

Pernon Debrot, 1583

Poland

Anna Chałupniczka

Anna Jasińska

Grzegorz

Jadwiga, 1681

Jan, 1727

Małgorzata Kupidarzyna

Marusza Staszkowa, 1656

Niewitecka

Oderyna, 1737

Wawrzyniec Dziad, 1719

GLOSSARY

Age of Enlightenment: An era in European history between the seventeenth and eighteenth century characterized by a focus on intellectual reasoning and a rejection of earlier superstitious belief.

Akelarre: The name given to the Witches' Sabbath in Basque folklore—translating to meadow (*larre*) of the billy goat (*aker*).

Apostasy: The act of rejecting one's previous religious beliefs. This may include verbal or physical acts of renunciation.

Astral Projection: The act of leaving the physical body and traveling in spirit form among the mundane world or into the astral realm.

Atavistic Resurgence: A term used by Kenneth Grant to describe a primal urge or longing for the divine source that lies at the beginning of all things.

Axis Mundi: The cosmic axis, or world tree, upon which the three realms are centered.

Bald Mountain: A generic name given to several mountains believed to be the site of Witches' Sabbaths.

Benevento: An Italian city believed to be a gathering spot for the Witches' Sabbath.

Black Mass: A ritual mocking the Catholic mass, characterized by inverted acts and symbols such as the desecration of the Eucharist.

Blåkulla: A mythical place in Swedish folklore said to be the gathering place for the Witches' Sabbath.

Blasphemy: A belief or action that is considered to be profane and disrespectful toward the Christian God or the Church itself.

Blocksberg: Another name for the Brocken.

Brocken: The highest peak of the Harz Mountains in Northern Germany, long believed to be a meeting place for the Witches' Sabbath.

Compass Round: A ritually created liminal working space in which Traditional Witches work magic and navigate the Otherworld.

Devil's Mark: A mark on the body of a Witch, given by the Devil in order to seal and signify the pact made upon initiation.

Diabolical Witchcraft: Both a concept and a crime consisting of a blend of sorcery and heresy.

Doñas de Fuera: Meaning "ladies from the outside." A group of supernatural women in Sicilian folklore, comparable to faeries, who would visit homes during the night to feast and bestow blessings upon the inhabitants.

Elfame: A Scottish term for the Faerie Realm.

Entheogen: A mind-altering substance used within a ritual context.

Esbat: A term introduced by Margaret Murray to describe a gathering of Witches for the purpose of working magic and engaging in celebratory acts, as opposed to the Sabbath, which was reserved for carrying out the rituals of the Witch-Cult.

Fair Folk: An euphemistic title given to the faeries, a specific type of spirit dwelling in the Midworld, often difficult to succinctly define or categorize.

Faerie Sabbath: A type of Sabbath appearing in the folklore of various cultures—primarily Irish, Scottish, and Italian—in which gatherings are presided over by faeries rather than the Devil.

Familiar Spirit: An umbrella term that refers to a spirit who comes to the aid of a Witch, often appearing in animal form.

Flying Ointment: A balm created from entheogenic herbs that, when applied to the body, helps facilitate hedge-crossing.

Furious Army/Das Wütende Heer: See *Wild Hunt.*

Genius Loci: The spirit of place who guards specific areas of land.

Hallow: The act of magically cleansing, blessing, or otherwise imbuing an object with magical power.

Hedge-Crossing: The process of venturing outside of one's body and traveling in spirit form into the Otherworld.

Heresy: Any religious beliefs or actions that stand in direct opposition to the teachings of the Catholic Church.

Herla/Helewin/Hellequin: A procession of penitent dead, often being tormented for their sins, common in twelfth-century folklore across England, France, and the Rhineland.

Ivan Kupala: A traditional Slavic holiday celebrated on the summer solstice, focused on purification and fertility.

Kia: A term coined by Austin Osman Spare to describe a universal consciousness or collective mind.

Land Wight: The spirits of nature who inhabit the plants, rocks, and other natural objects.

Łysa Góra: Meaning "Bald Mountain." A hill in the Świętokrzyskie Mountains of Poland believed to be a gathering place for the Witches' Sabbath.

Malefica: Any act of magic used to cause harm or destruction.

Man in Black: Another name for the Witch Father, particularly associated with his presence at the Sabbath.

Maundy Thursday: A Christian holy day, falling on the Thursday before Easter, commemorating the Washing of the Feet and the Last Supper.

Midworld: The physical world of humans as well as the hidden landscape behind it, which is inhabited by spirits such as the Faerie Folk.

Mighty Dead: A group of ancestors made up of Witches and other magical practitioners who have passed on.

Modern Witchcraft Revival: A period of increased public interest in the practice of Witchcraft occurring from the mid-twentieth century to the present day.

Mountain of Venus: Also known as Venusberg, a mountain in English and German folklore believed to be the dwelling place of various supernatural women, including the Roman goddess Venus, from whom the mountain receives its name.

Operative Witchcraft: A term used by Margaret Murray to describe practical acts of Witchcraft, such as spellcraft and divination, often performed alone.

Otherworld: The world of spirits, divided into three realms: the Upperworld, Midworld, and Underworld.

Poppet: A magical doll used to represent the target of a spell or ritual.

Puy-de-Dôme: A lava dome in Central France believed to have been a meeting place for the Witches' Sabbath.

Reina de las Hadas: The Italian Faerie Queen, leader of the *doñas de fuera*.

Ritual Witchcraft: A term used by Margaret Murray to describe religious acts of Witchcraft, such as the carrying out of specific rituals to honor deities.

Sabbat: A modern ritual celebration marking the changing of the seasons.

Sabbath: A nocturnal meeting of Witches and spirits occurring in the Otherworld.

Sabbath Queen: A Witch or some spirit chosen by the Devil to preside over the Sabbath alongside him.

Sabbatic Craft: A tradition of Witchcraft established by the late Andrew Chumbley, based on the imagery and resulting gnosis of the Witches' Sabbath.

Sorcery: The practice of magic, traditionally believed to involve working with demons.

Stang: A bifurcated ritual staff used as an altar to the Witch Father and to direct magical power.

Strix: A mythological, birdlike creature—sometimes thought to be a shape-shifting woman or Witch—who was believed to murder and devour babies.

Synagogue: A sacred gathering place for Jewish people to engage in religious observation. The term has historically been inappropriately used to describe gatherings of Witches, demonstrating early anti-Semitic attitudes.

Traditional Witchcraft: An umbrella term that covers a vast array of non-Wiccan practices that are inspired by folklore. These practices may be viewed as religious or spiritual depending upon the group or individual practitioner. Traditional Witches focus on the use of magic, connecting with the natural world and working with various spirits in both the physical realm and the Otherworld.

Trance State: An altered state of consciousness in which one is somewhere between wakefulness and sleep.

Transcendental Sorcery: A term coined by Andrew Chumbley to describe the combination of operative forms of magic with ritual workings aimed at achieving spiritual gnosis.

Treading the Mill: A ritual involving repetitive circling around a fixed central object with one's head turned to the side and slightly tilted back. It is used to alter consciousness and raise personal magical power.

Underworld: The lower realm of the Otherworld, where the ancestors reside. Often associated with the powers of emotions.

Upperworld: The upper realm of the Otherworld, where the gods reside. Often associated with the powers of the mind.

Virtues: The magical powers contained within natural objects such as plants, stones, animals, planets, and so on.

Waldensians: Members of a Christian religious movement deemed heretical by the Catholic Church in 1184 and later associated with Witchcraft.

Walpurgisnacht: The night of April 30, the eve of the Christian feast day of Saint Walpurga, a night when Witches in German folklore were believed to gather for their Sabbath.

Wheel of the Year: A modern system of seasonal ritual celebrations made up of eight sabbats—Samhain, the winter solstice (Yule), Imbolc, the spring equinox (Ostara), Beltane, the summer solstice (Litha), Lammas, and the fall equinox (Mabon).

Wicca: A specific subset of Witchcraft, founded by Gerald Gardner during the late 1940s and early 1950s.

Wild Hunt: A retinue of ghosts, faeries, and other beings who are said to take to the sky on stormy nights, collecting the souls of the dead and warning of impending disasters.

Witchcraft Act of 1735: A law passed by the Parliament of the Kingdom of Great Britain under which the practice of Witchcraft, while still illegal, was no longer punishable by death.

Witch-Cult Hypothesis: A belief that those persecuted during the European Witch trials were actually members of a once-widespread Pagan religion.

Witch Father: The archetypal masculine deity within Traditional Witchcraft.

Witch Mother: The archetypal feminine deity within Traditional Witchcraft.

Witch Name: A new name given to a Witch by the Devil upon their initiation.

World Tree: Another name for the axis mundi.

Zos: A term coined by Austin Osman Spare to describe the physical body and mundane mind.

RECOMMENDED READING

Ecstasies: Deciphering the Witches' Sabbath by Carlo Ginzburg
A true classic, Ginzburg's book was—and continues to be—a pivotal study on the early development of the Witches' Sabbath. While the text itself is rather academic and quite dense, it's well worth the read!

The Triumph of the Moon by Ronald Hutton
Hutton's book has been a real game-changer for many practitioners, as it provides a well-rounded, academically inclined history of modern Witchcraft and Paganism. If you're looking to learn more about the Modern Witchcraft Revival, this book is a must read.

The Witches' Ointment by Thomas Hatsis
Filled with fascinating stories, this book lays out the historical development of Witches' flying ointment. I cannot recommend this book enough for anyone who wishes to know more about *unguentum sabbati*.

Witch's Wheel of the Year by Jason Mankey
Mankey's book offers readers not only a look into the history and folklore of each of the Wiccan Sabbats, but a sundry of beautifully written rituals as well. By far one of my favorite texts on the Wheel of Year to date.

Encyclopedia of Spirits: The Ultimate Guide to the Magic of Saints, Angels, Fairies, Demons, and Ghosts by Judika Illes

With over a thousand pages of information, Illes's encyclopedia is an impressive and essential source on the many different types of spirits. If you are in need of assistance when it comes to learning more about Otherworldly beings, you will surely find it within this book.

To Fly by Night: Craft of the Hedgewitch, edited by Veronica Cummer

A fantastic anthology regarding the art of spirit flight. If you are looking to learn more about the various aspects of hedge-crossing, this is an excellent book, as it contains dozens of essays written by a diverse set of practitioners.

The Crooked Path: An Introduction to Traditional Witchcraft by Kelden

My previous book is a good place to start if you are new to Traditional Witchcraft. Among many other topics, in the book you will find additional information regarding the Otherworld as well as working with various spirits, such as deities, ancestors, familiars, and faeries.

The Witch-Cult in Western Europe by Margaret Murray

While Murray's work has been largely discredited, her book has—and continues to be—highly influential when it comes to modern Witchcraft. If nothing else, Murray's text is a valuable collection of quotes from Witch Trial transcripts.

Invoking the Akelarre by Emma Wilby

Discussing the Witch Trials that took place in the Basque religion, this book explores the ways in which confessional material was often influenced by both the persecutors and the accused. Wilby does a phenomenal job highlighting the voices of the accused Witches and shedding light on the folkloric sources of their Sabbath narratives.

Witchcraft in Europe: 400–1700 **edited by Alan Charles Kors and Edward Peters**

Containing dozens of historical documents, this text provides an in-depth look at the thoughts and beliefs of the persecutors, writers, and other authorities leading up to, during, and after the European Witch Trials. This text was invaluable in writing *The Witches' Sabbath*.

BIBLIOGRAPHY

"Agnes (Bigis) Cairnes (5/4/1659)." Survey of Scottish Witchcraft Database. Accessed February 5, 2021. http://witches.shca.ed.ac.uk/index .cfm?fuseaction=home.caserecord&caseref=C%2FEGD%2F792& search_type=searchaccused&search_string=lastname%3Dcairnes.

Ankarloo, Bengt, and Gustav Henningsen, eds. *Early Modern European Witchcraft*. Oxford: Claredon Press, 1990.

Authority, *The Lawes against VVitches, and Conivration*. London: R. W., 1645. Ann Arbor, MI: Text Creation Partnership, 2011. https://quod .lib.umich.edu/e/eebo/A88821.0001.001/1:2.2?rgn=div2;view =fulltext.

Baker, Phil. *Austin Osman Spare*. Reprint, Berkeley, CA: North Atlantic Books, 2014.

Barber, Malcolm. "Lepers, Jews and Moslems: The Plot to Overthrow Christendom in 1321," *History* 66, no. 216 (1981): 1–17. https://doi .org/10.1111/j.1468-229X.1981.tb01356.x.

Bodin, Jean. *On the Demon-Mania of Witches*. Translated by Randy A. Scott. Toronto: Centre for Reformation and Renaissance Studies, 1995.

Boguet, Henry. *An Examen of Witches*. Mineola, NY: Dover Publications, 2009.

Briggs, Robin. *Witches & Neighbors*. New York: Penguin, 1996.

———. *The Witches of Lorraine*. Oxford: Oxford University Press, 2007.

Broedel, Hans Peter. "Fifteenth-Century Witch Beliefs." In *The Oxford Handbook of Witchcraft in Early Modern Europe and Colonial America*, edited by Brian Levack, 32–49. Oxford: Oxford University Press, 2013.

Buckland, Raymond. *Witchcraft from the Inside*. St. Paul, MN: Llewellyn Publications, 1995.

Burchard of Worms. *Decretorum Liber Decimus*. In *Patrologiae cursus completus*... Vol. 140. Paris: Jacques-Paul Migne, 1880.

Burns, Robert. "Tam o' Shanter." Poetry Foundation. Accessed February 5, 2021. https://www.poetryfoundation.org/poems/43815/tam-o -shanter.

Burr, George L. "Review of Margaret Murray's *The Witch-Cult in Western Europe*." *The American Historical Review* 27, no. 4 (1922), 780–83. https://doi.org/10.1086/ahr/27.4.780.

Burr, George Lincoln, ed. *Narratives of the New England Witchcraft Cases*. Mineola, NY: Dover Publications, 2012.

Carmichael, James. "Newes from Scotland, declaring the damnable life and death of Doctor Fian a notable sorcerer [...]." London: [E. Allde?], c. 1542. Ann Arbor, MI: Text Creation Partnership, 2011. https://quod.lib.umich.edu/e/eebo/A00710.0001.001/1:4?rgn=div1 ;view=fulltext.

Cohn, Norman. *Europe's Inner Demons*. Chicago: University of Chicago Press, 2000.

Craigie, William A. *Scandinavian Folk-Lore: Illustrations of the Traditional Beliefs of the Northern Peoples*. London: Alexander Gardner, 1896.

De Lancre, Pierre. *On the Inconstancy of Witches*. Translated by Harriet Stone and Gerhild Scholz Williams. Tempe: Arizona Center for Medieval and Renaissance Studies, 2006.

Essex Institute. *Historical Collections of the Essex Institute*. Vol. 3. Salem, MA: G. M. Whipple and A. A. Smith, 1861.

Etymological Dictionary of Basque. Compiled by R. L. Trask. Brighton, England: University of Sussex, 2008.

Fergusson, R. Menzies. "The Witches of Alloa." *The Scottish Historical Review* 4, no. 13 (1906): 40–48. https://www.jstor.org/stable/25517800.

Gage, Matilda Joslyn. *Woman, Church and State.* New York: The Truth Seeker Company, 1893.

Gardner, Gerald. *The Meaning of Witchcraft.* York Beach, ME: Weiser, 2004.

———. *Witchcraft Today.* New York: Citadel Press, 2004.

Gary, Gemma. *Traditional Witchcraft: A Cornish Book of Ways.* London: Troy Books Publishing, 2008.

Ginzburg, Carlo. *Ecstasies: Deciphering the Witches' Sabbath.* Translated by Raymond Rosenthal. New York: Pantheon Books, 1991.

———. *The Night Battles: Witchcraft and Agrarian Cults in the Sixteenth and Seventeenth Centuries.* Translated by John Tedeschi and Anne C. Tedeschi. Baltimore, MD: John Hopkins University Press, 2013.

Glanvill, Joseph. *Saducismus Triumphatus: Or, Full and Plain Evidence Concerning Witches and Apparitions.* London: S. Lownds, 1681.

Goethe, Johann Wolfgang von. *Faust.* Translated by Alice Raphael. Norwalk, CT: The Heritage Press, 1959.

Grant, Kenneth, and Steffi Grant. *Hidden Lore: The Carfax Monographs.* London: Skoob Books Publishing, 1989.

Grimassi, Raven. *Old World Witchcraft.* San Francisco: Weiser Books, 2011.

Grimm, Jacob. *Teutonic Mythology.* Vol. 3. Translated by James Steven Stallybrass. London: George Bell & Sons, 1883.

Harland, John, and Thomas Turner Wilkinson. *Lancashire Folk-Lore.* London: Frederick Warne and Co., 1867.

Hatsis, Thomas. *The Witches' Ointment.* Rochester, VT: Park Street Press, 2015.

Henningsen, Guztav, ed. *The Salazar Documents*. Leiden: Brill, 2004.

Heselton, Philip. *Doreen Valiente: Witch*. Woodbury, MN: Llewellyn Publications, 2016.

Hole, Christina. *Witchcraft in England*. London: B. T. Batsford, 1947.

Howard, Michael. *Children of Cain*. Richmond Vista, CA: Three Hands Press, 2011.

Hutton, Ronald. *Triumph of the Moon*. Oxford: Oxford University Press, 1999.

———. *The Witch*. New Haven, CT: Yale University Press, 2017.

Illes, Judika. *The Element Encyclopedia of Witchcraft*. London: HarperCollins Publishers, 2005.

James VI. *Daemonologie*. Edited by G. B. Harrison. London: John Lane, 1922–1926. Electronic reproduction by John Bruno Hare. Internet Sacred Text Archive. Accessed February 5, 2021. https://www.sacred-texts.com/pag/kjd/index.htm.

Jansen, Katherine L., Joanna Drell, and Frances Andrews, eds. *Medieval Italy: Texts in Translation*. Philadelphia: University of Pennsylvania Press, 2009.

King Clovis. "Pactus Legis Salicae." In *The Laws of the Salian Franks*. Edited and translated by Katherine Fischer Drew. Philadelphia: University of Pennsylvania Press, 1991.

Kinloch, George Ritchie. *Reliquiae Antiquae Scoticae*. Edinburgh: Thomas G. Stevenson, 1848.

Klaniczay, Gábor, and Éva Pócs, eds. *Witchcraft Mythologies and Persecutions*. Vol. 3 of *Demons, Spirits, Witches*. New York: Central European University Press, 2008.

Kors, Alan Charles, and Edward Peters, eds. *Witchcraft in Europe: 400–1700*. Philadelphia: University of Pennsylvania, 2001.

Kramer, Heinrich, and Jacob Sprenger. *The Malleus Maleficarum*. Translated by Montague Summers. Mineola, NY: Dover Publications, 1971.

Lea, Henry Charles. *A History of the Inquisition of the Middle Ages*. Vol. 2 New York: Harper & Brothers, 1888.

Le Beau, Bryan F. *The Story of the Salem Witch Trials*. New York: Routledge, 2016.

Lecouteux, Claude. *Phantom Armies of the Night*. Translated by Jon E. Graham. Rochester, VT: Inner Traditions, 2011.

Leland, Charles Godfrey. *Aradia: Or the Gospel of the Witches*. London: Troy Books, 2018.

Levack, Brian P., ed. *The Witchcraft Sourcebook*. London: Routledge, 2015.

Lorris, Guillaume de, and Jean de Meun. *Romance of the Rose*. Translated by Charles Dahlberg. Princeton, NJ: Princeton University Press, 1995.

Mankey, Jason. *Witch's Wheel of Year*. Woodbury, MN: Llewellyn Publications, 2019.

Maxwell-Stuart, P. G. *Witch Beliefs and Witch Trials in the Middle Ages*. London: Continuum, 2011.

Michelet, Jules. *La Sorcière*. Translated by Lionel James Trotter. London: Simpkin, Marshall, and Co., 1863.

Monter, E. William. *Witchcraft in France and Switzerland*. Ithaca, NY: Cornell University Press, 1976.

Motz, Lotte. "The Winter Goddess: Percht, Holda, and Related Figures." *Folklore* 95, no. 2 (1984): 151–66.

Murray, Margaret A. *The God of the Witches*. Oxford: Oxford University Press, 1970.

———. *The Witch-Cult in Western Europe*. Oxford: Clarendon Press, 1921. Reprint, New York: Barnes and Noble, 1996.

Ovid. *The Fasti of Ovid*. Translated by John Benson Rose. London: Dorrell and Sons, 1866.

Pearson, Nigel. *Treading the Mill*. London: Troy Books Publishing, 2017.

Penczak, Christopher. *The Inner Temple of Witchcraft*. St. Paul, MN: Llewellyn Publications, 2002.

Pepper, Elizabeth, and John Wilcock. *Magical and Mystical Sites: Europe and the British Isles*. Grand Rapids, MI: Phanes Press, 2000.

Pitcairn, Robert. *Ancient Criminal Trials in Scotland*. Vol. 1. Edinburgh: Ballantyne and Co., 1833.

Pitcairn, Robert. *Ancient Criminal Trials in Scotland*. Vol. 3. Edinburgh: Ballantyne and Co., 1833.

Porta, Giambattista della. *Natural Magick*. Obernkirchen, Germany: Black Letter Press, 2020.

A Relation of the Diabolical Practices of Above Twenty Wizards and Witches of the Sheriffdom of Renfrew in the Kingdom of Scotland. London: Hugh Newman, 1697.

Remy, Nicolas. *Demonolatry*. Translated by E. A. Ashwin. Mineola, NY: Dover Publications, 2008.

Richards, Jeffrey. *Sex, Dissidence and Damnation*. New York: Routledge, 1994.

Roberts, Alexander, and James Donaldson, eds. *Ante-Nicene Fathers*. Vol. 4, *Tertullian*. Peabody, MA: Hendrickson Publishers, 1995.

Roper, Lyndal. *Witch Craze*. New Haven, CT: Yale University Press, 2004.

Ross, Richard S., III. *Before Salem: Witch Hunting in the Connecticut River Valley, 1647–1663*. Jefferson, NC: McFarland & Company, 2017.

Scott, Walter. *Letters on Demonology and Witchcraft*. London: George Routledge and Sons, 1884.

Sharpe, Charles Kirkpatrick. *A Historical Account of the Belief in Witchcraft in Scotland*. London: Hamilton, Adams & Co., 1884.

Schulke, Daniel A., ed. *Opuscula Magica*. Vol. 2, *Essays on Witchcraft and Crooked Path Sorcery*. Richmond Vista, CA: Three Hands Press, 2011.

The Spalding Club. *Miscellany of the Spalding Club*. Vol. 1. Aberdeen, Scotland: Spalding Club, 1841.

Spare, Austin Osman. "Zoëtic Grimoire of Zos." In *Zos Speaks!*, ed. Kenneth Grant and Steffi Grant. London: Fulger Limited, 1998.

"SWP No. 009: William Barker, Sr." Salem Witch Trials Documentary Archive and Transcription Project. August 25, 1692. Accessed February 5, 2021. http://salem.lib.virginia.edu/n9.html.

"SWP No. 022: George Burroughs Executed, August 19, 1692." Salem Witch Trials Documentary Archive and Transcription Project. August 30, 1692. Accessed February 5, 2021. http://salem.lib.virginia.edu/n22.html.

"SWP No. 087: Mary Lacey, Jr." Salem Witch Trials Documentary Archive and Transcription Project. July 20, 1692. Accessed February 5, 2021. http://salem.lib.virginia.edu/n87.html.

"SWP No. 096: Mary Osgood." Salem Witch Trials Documentary Archive and Transcription Project. September 8, 1692. Accessed February 5, 2021. http://salem.lib.virginia.edu/n96.html.

"SWP No. 128: Mary Toothaker." Salem Witch Trials Documentary Archive and Transcription Project. June 4, 1692, and July 30, 1692. Accessed February 5, 2021. http://salem.lib.virginia.edu/n128.html.

"Tam o' Shanter," Burns Country, accessed February 5, 2021, http://www.robertburns.org/encyclopedia/TamOShanter.23.shtml.

Vitalis, Ordericus. *The Ecclesiastical History of England and Normandy.* Translated by Thomas Forester. Vol. 2. London: H. G. Bohn, 1854.

Wilby, Emma. *Invoking the Akelarre: Voices of the Accused in the Basque Witch-Craze, 1609–1614.* Chicago: Sussex Academic Press, 2019.

Wyporska, Wanda. *Witchcraft in Early Modern Poland 1500–1800.* New York: Palgrave Macmillian, 2013.

Younger Pliny. *The Letters of the Younger Pliny.* Translated by John B. Firth. 2nd series. London: Walter Scott, 1900. https://babel.hathitrust.org/cgi/pt?id=umn.31951002237967y&view=1up&seq=296&skin=2021.

To Write to the Author

If you wish to contact the author or would like more information about this book, please write to the author in care of Llewellyn Worldwide Ltd. and we will forward your request. Both the author and the publisher appreciate hearing from you and learning of your enjoyment of this book and how it has helped you. Llewellyn Worldwide Ltd. cannot guarantee that every letter written to the author can be answered, but all will be forwarded. Please write to:

Kelden
℅ Llewellyn Worldwide
2143 Wooddale Drive
Woodbury, MN 55125-2989
Please enclose a self-addressed stamped envelope for reply,
or $1.00 to cover costs. If outside the U.S.A., enclose
an international postal reply coupon.

Many of Llewellyn's authors have websites with additional information and resources. For more information, please visit our website at http://www.llewellyn.com.